LETTERS & PAMPHLETS

Fulgentius Ferrandus

Translated by: D.P. Curtin

LETTERS & PAMPHLETS

Copyright @ 2024 Dalcassian Press

All rights reserved. No part of this publication may be reproduced, distributed, or transmitted in any form or by any means, including photocopying, recording, or other electronic or mechanical methods, without the prior written permission of the publisher, except in the case of brief quotations embodied in critical reviews and certain other non-commercial uses permitted by copyright law. For permission request, write to Dalcassian Press at dalcassianpublishing at gmail.com

ISBN: 979-8-8693-8328-0 (Paperback)

Library of Congress Control Number:
Author: Curtin, D.P. (1985-)

Printed by Ingram Content Group, 1 Ingram Blvd, La Vergne, Tennessee

First printing edition 2024.

LETTERS & PAMPHLETS

LETTERS & PAMPHLETS

LETTERS & PAMPHLETS

EPISTLE I. Ferrandus the deacon Fulgentius raises two questions, concerning the salvation of an Ethiopian catechumen, who was baptized when he was already mentally burdened by the force of disease, and who had not received the eucharist of the dead. Receiving the most blessed Lord and with all veneration Father Fulgentius the bishop, Ferrandus the deacon, greeting in the Lord.

1. Those who are in need of earthly resources, nor of long-term continuous labor, or the diligence of honest art, etc.

EPISTLE II. Ferrandus Fulgentio, proposing five questions. Looking at the most blessed Lord and with all veneration the holy father Fulgentius the bishop, Ferrandus the deacon salutes the Lord.

1. I often wanted to ask many questions with the feeling of learning: but I addressed the absent teacher with frequent letters, the rarity of porters prevented me from the distance of the journey, etc.

EPISTLE III. TO ANATOLIUM, DEACON OF THE CITY OF ROME.

Of the two natures in Christ: and that one in the Trinity may be said to have been born and suffered.

1. After the letter of the blessed Pope Leo, and the salutary decrees of the council of Chalcedon, holy brother Anatolius, there is no need to convince Eutyches of the perfidy once condemned by a fuller discussion. So let the profane inventor of the infamous heresy lie buried in his ashes. Once the authority of the judging priests struck him with the thunderbolt of anathema: what need is there again for a lifeless corpse to be infected with the sword of truth? At the same time, learning that lacks the light of reason hides the prison of perpetual silence. Sometimes the worst doctrines, while they are uttered as if they were to be attacked, disturb the hearts of the simple with a pestilent poison. It is better not to know these things, and to keep the Catholic faith inviolable by supplicating profane novelties: by remaining in its original firmness, which are also strengthened by synodal definitions. Or if you think it more necessary to always refute the lies of the heretics, open my tongue with the keys of your command: I will hasten, as far as grace can grant, to obey the gentle commander. Provide the right hand of good favor and protect the bare breast with the shield of prayer, to enter the field of free combat with me, if it so pleases: against the wicked ranks, of those who are wrongly slain, who try to claim the harmful inheritance, he will fight without effort. Neither weapons are new to them, nor camps. They still want to beat down the walls of apostolic preaching with the spikes which the standard-bearer of the heretics hurled in vain, becoming a prey to the birds of heaven. But two, as far as we have read, Eutyches carried the weapons of his own error, whence, coming out from the Dominican side, he desired to wound the Church like a treacherous soldier. For denying that Mary, ever a virgin, by the working power of the Holy Spirit, ministered the matter of her flesh to the only-begotten God to be born from human entrails, he refused to admit the consubstantial Son to his mother; and for this reason, severing the integrity of Catholic unity, with a noxious attack of the twisted thorn, doubting to believe in the two substances of the incarnate

Word, he completely severed one. But he who fights with the weapons of justice on the right and on the left, has indeed weakened one fatally damaging sentence, immediately emptied of his strength, so that you can hardly find anyone who dares to deny the truth of the mother's body of the Lord Jesus Christ. Indeed, the singularity of one person frightens the most unwary from the idea of two substances. However, we respond to both propositions, lest we be seen to have despised your government; and following the rule of the Fathers, we will also speak to you well known to the fearless.

2. For I trust that I know your skill well, because if, according to what the heretic thought, nay, rather, he lost it, the flesh of the Word of God according to the flesh of that which is born of the flesh of the Virgin is pronounced foreign, without cause the Son of God is also asserted to have become the son of man. For how is he naturally a son of man, who has no origin from man? Does it have any origin from man, if the conception in the womb of a virgin did not draw flesh from flesh? It is agreed that without the seed of his father, his mother's bowels fertilized him; but what will be the fecundity of Mary, if it is not from that which is born through her flesh? The Word became flesh and dwelt among us, says John the evangelist (Chapter 1, v. 14). Are you wondering where the meat is made from? Let Blessed Paul answer your inquiry: After the fullness of time had come, God sent forth his Son made of woman (Gal. 4:4). Therefore God sent His Son, that is, God made His Word flesh; but whence? From a woman If, therefore, the Word was made flesh from a woman, the flesh of the Word was undoubtedly taken from a woman. This woman is always called the Virgin Mary, a woman by the name of the sex, who therefore, saved from shame, conceived and gave birth to God, because from her God received the truth of the flesh by becoming man. Otherwise, if the Creator had fashioned for himself the flesh of a new kind to be created, either out of nothing, or from wherever he wished, it would have had to appear suddenly to the eyes of mortals, rather than endure for ten months the hospitality of a small stomach, the size of which heaven is not sufficient. Why was it necessary that Joseph, the faithful bridegroom, seeing the most chaste spouse, before they met, became a parent, suspected adultery, because he did not yet know the heavenly mystery? The only-begotten God would be man, just as man was without a father, so without a mother, if he had nothing to receive from his mother. The son of no man would come to the sons of men, if he had nothing

in common with the sons of men. This opinion is too objectionable, the shame of the truth oppresses the one who considers it any longer. A virgin gives birth to a son to the astonishment of all, and the entrails of the begetting are supposed to have remained barren, because nothing of themselves penetrates into the members of the newborn? The earth produces insensible plants, and no one denies to them the quality of earthly substance: Mary conceives the Son of God, gives birth to the Son of God, and does she not recognize in him the property of her substance? He will certainly be judged to sin more tolerably, because, suspecting that the Lord Jesus Christ received nothing from Mary, he is silent even when he was born; for he does a great injury to birth, whosoever makes any difference between the substance of the procreator and the begotten; reproving this worst blasphemy to the Doctor of the Gentiles, knowing that the principles of the Epistle should be adorned more clearly with the title of true faith, he began to edify the Romans with this speech: He was made of the seed of David according to the flesh; who is predestined to be the Son of God in power according to the spirit of sanctification, from the resurrection of Jesus Christ our Lord from the dead (Rom. 1:1-4).

3. Let the heretic now say how the Son of God was made of the seed of David according to the flesh. Joseph surely dreamed nothing of Mary, to whom it is said by the angel: The Holy Spirit will come upon you, and the power of the Most High will overshadow you. Why is Christ called again from the seed of David? Why is he, born among men without human seed, said to have been made of the seed of David? It is not necessary to consider the power of this preaching lightly, nor in vain. For the Apostle is mindful of his doctrine, and likewise in another place also admonishes his dearest disciple Timothy: Remember, you who say, that Jesus Christ rose from the dead from the seed of David according to my gospel (II Tim. 2:8). Who, therefore, planted the seed of David in the substance of humanity at his birth? Where could it become of the seed of David? If he was born without a man to his father, then by what reason would he become of the seed of David, unless he had taken flesh from a mother who belonged to the seed of David? For Mary is of the seed of David, and Christ of Mary's flesh; although without marital seed, yet with the property of nature. Because of this, the Psalmist sings with a prophetic spirit: The Lord will give kindness, and our land will give its fruit (Ps. 84:13), because in the evident substance of the flesh accepted by her, Mary gave birth to her Lord. For if the

flesh of Christ were born from another place, the earth, that is, Mary, would by no means give its own fruit, but that of another; nor again would the holy apostle signify that the seed of Abraham was Christ, when he said thus: The promises were made to Abraham, and to his seed. He does not say: and to the seeds, as if in many; but, as in one: and your seed, which is Christ (Gal. 3:16). What is more open? What is more obvious? Was not Christ also the seed of Abraham, how from the seed of David because of Mary, through Mary, from Mary? The impious debater takes away from Christ the matter of the flesh which Mary served, and teaches how Christ is the seed of Abraham, or how he was made from the seed of David. Did it seem that Abraham, being full of faith, foresaw what was to come, by a superfluous sacrament, was confining himself to the vernacular proper? He would certainly say: Touch my breast bright with holy thoughts; touch the hands enriched with the gift of innocence; touch the head of no one liable to crime. Why are the more honorable members omitted, and the one who is about to swear forced to place his hand under the sole of his thigh? Something great was hidden in this thigh: for the flesh of Christ was hidden there, which had been born from his offspring. Therefore, by the touch of the thigh, a terrible oath is uttered by the God of heaven: because the God of heaven was to be born according to the flesh, as are usually born whom the generation signified by the name of the thigh assigns to conform to those of whom they are formed.

4. Therefore the flesh of Christ was taken from the mother, therefore it is more true; but it is plainly holy, because it is purified by the union of the divinity. In the flesh of Christ is the nature of our flesh, but no fault of the nature is found. Thus the flesh of Christ is both like and unlike the flesh of Mary: like, because it drew its origin from thence; unlike, because he did not thereby contract the contagion of a vitiated origin; similar, because, although voluntary, he nevertheless felt true infirmities; unlike, because he committed no iniquities at all, either through will or ignorance: similar, because he was susceptible and mortal; unlike, because it is undefiled, and gives life even to the dead: similar in kind, unlike in merit: similar in appearance, unlike in virtue: similar, because it is a similitude of the sin of the flesh, saying to the Apostle: God sent his Son in the similitude of the flesh of sin (Rom. 8:3). Behold, how much the flesh of Christ is taught by Mary the cause of a new existence, naturally attained according to the solemnity of human birth, sequestered by the necessity of

marital intercourse, so that it is not indeed the flesh of sin, because it is the flesh of God; yet let it be the similitude of the flesh of sin, because it was truly born of mortal flesh: also by virtue of mortal flesh, because it drew matter from mortal flesh. For he who has no sin at all in his flesh, by what door would voluntary death enter, unless it were born of his flesh, in whom could sin be, and death through sin? We will explain this more fully in clear words. Christ's flesh was not conceived in iniquities: for what reason then does it seem to have experienced the condition of death? We clearly know that the Son of God died for us, not by necessity, but willingly. However, the holy apostle is a witness to the truth, truthfully saying: Through one man sin entered the world, and death through sin (Rom. 5:1). Sin did not enter into that flesh of Christ. Whence death, though voluntary, entered, except because divine power caused him to be born without sin, and divine mercy caused him to die without sin? Nevertheless, by the fact that there was a maternal substance in him, it will be proved by no better document that Christ had flesh from a mortal mother, except by the punishment of death. Grace to him who, taking the nature of human flesh without fault, did not, however, remove the fault without punishment: he ended the punishment and healed the nature, so that it has a common nature with us. For it was necessary for him, like a priest, to receive from us what he would offer for us; But if he did not receive from Mary the material of the flesh, he did not receive from us what he could offer for us. and how could he perform the eternal function of a priest? Our priest had to give us a sacrifice to sacrifice to God; But the only begotten Son of God the Father, our priest in mortal flesh, did not offer gold, nor silver, nor the blood of goats, but his own body. Our victim, then, is his body; and if he received his body, he therefore received a body from us; and this he received then, when Saint Mary conceived him. He must therefore be believed to be consubstantial with the mother, just as he is consubstantial with the Father. The consubstantial one also conquered the devil for us as well: therefore from the depths of captivity he lifted up the whole race of men mercifully. Adam was defeated, persuaded by the flattery of women to eat from the forbidden tree; Christ won, being hanged on a wooden gallows by Jewish fury and cries. What good is Adam's victory in Christ, if his substance is not in Christ? And how could this be done, unless the Virgin Mary had thus given birth to him, so as to provide him without iniquity with the material of the flesh, in which he could be temporarily born and suffer?

5. In this way faith reminds us that the truth must be felt, that Christ had a true body, not airy, not fantastic, not formed from elsewhere, but fleshly; taken from the flesh of the Virgin, though not sown carnally, but quickened by the inspiration of the rational soul; such as we are, without sin; such that the devil was deceived into swallowing the hook, mistaking it for meat. For unless the devil saw in Christ the Savior a true body and consubstantial with his mother, he would not dare to tempt or kill. Moreover, in whom he saw nothing of his own, the Lord himself telling his disciples: Behold, the ruler of this world will come and find in me nothing (John 14:30), certainly of sin: for in him the mother's nature was full, that is ours; as though he owed him something, that ancient moneylender of sin invaded, crucified, and killed; and by undue exaction he lost all that was due to him: he was justly defeated and justly punished; because that flesh conquered in Christ, which had been conquered in Adam. For this was the justice of God, that through that flesh the author of death should be overcome in Christ, which he had overcome in Adam, and that flesh should die without sin, that all sin might be blotted out, which had been dead by sin: by the marvelous working grace of the Saviour, that death might become the medicine of the punishment of sin afterwards of sinners. Adam sinned, and died, and bound all his posterity with the fetters of eternal death; Christ died, and because he had not sinned, he freed all sinners from the dominion of death. If, then, there were another nature of the flesh, in which Christ had not sinned and died, the devil would be overcome, not by justice, but by power. But it was necessary to conquer by justice. But it was justice itself, that the Redeemer should come in her flesh, which the tempter had caused to remain subject to punishment. That is why God wanted to become man, so that man could easily be reconciled to God through the man God. For a great separation had taken place between the just God and sinful man; nor was God close to man in substance, nor was the righteous sinner embraced in grace. God, therefore, humbling himself, became a just man, and God was reconciled to sinful man. God became what was not, man; and he became man in the same way that he was not, just. But if the just God were to become a just man by such a chance that he would not belong to the substance of which man had been a sinner, nor would he have anything peculiar to the sinner's substance, man would remain a sinner forever. But now, having been made partakers of grace through the likeness of substance, we have been justified in that only-begotten God who willed for us to become a man like us. Hence even the most holy Paul, dealing with the mystery of the incarnation, speaks thus of

Christ to the Hebrews: For he never apprehended the angels, but he apprehended the seed of Abraham. Wherefore he had to be like his brethren in all things, that he might become a merciful and faithful priest to God, that he might atone for the transgressions of the people (Heb. 2:16-17). Who is able to explain this chapter with words worthy of understanding? He ought, he said, to be like his brothers in all things. O ignorant defender of foolish heresies! How could Christ be like his brothers in all things, if he had been unlike in substance? How will it be similar at all in substance, except by receiving flesh from Mary? Let the profane heart cease from such thoughts. He who denies that Christ, the true Son of God, miraculously assumed the true truth of the flesh from the true mother, wants to completely nullify the work of the mediator. For he is a mediator only of two, whom he separates from one another, then he himself joins rightly and firmly by existing as the mediator, if he is similar in substance to both, whom he causes to draw near to him by grace. And Christ exists as the mediator of God and men, as the vessel of election insinuates: One God, one and mediator of God and men, the man Christ Jesus (1 Tim. 2:5); if man is not thus of man, how is God of God? If man is not consubstantial with his mother, how is he consubstantial with God the Father? If his divine substance is in common with God, but his human substance is not supposed to be in common with men, he either bears the person, or carries out the office of an unsuccessful mediator. Nevertheless, because he is such a mediator that he is a true mediator, he is consubstantial with both Father and Mother, and God and men; and by this means not of one substance, but of two substances, because it can never be the mediator of one substance.

6. See, most holy brother, how secretly we have entered the threshold of another question, opening the doors with truth itself. For while we wish, through the office of mediator, to discover, or rather to prove, the propriety, likeness, and truth of the human substance, lest we cut off the fecundity of the Virgin mother, the clear distinction of the two substances shines forth in the named and considered mediator. Because of course there is one mediator, if you consider the person to whom the name of mediator has come, and the mediator existing between two things of unlike substance, can only fulfill the office of mediator through two substances. For whose person and nature are one, he can in no way be or be said to be a mediator between two substances, because with that substance, to which his one nature is in the least joined, he is entirely

destitute of the office of mediator. and then he is a true mediator, when, in order to unite the division of two unlike substances, he carries on a substantial communion with both; by the communion itself removing the division, that both may be one; Let us consider this more fully in our mediator, namely the Lord Christ; which indeed is truly one person (for it is not fitting that there should be two persons of one mediator), yet it is not of one nature, although of one mediator. Because this one nature (since it is the mediator between God and men) it will certainly be common either with God or with men. For absolutely, no matter how much the heretic claims, one nature cannot be common to God and men, because God is the creator, we are creatures; God is eternal, we are temporal; God is incomprehensible, we are comprehensible; God without place, we in place; God is infinite and immeasurable, we are limited and determined. Again, therefore, I say confidently: if the nature of Christ is one, it can be common either with God the Father, or with men; God and men can never be common. Now Christ is of one substance with the Father, which the Greeks call homousion, according to the absolute profession of the Council of Nicaea. Therefore the one nature of Christ Jesus is common to him with the Father. And in what way is it possible for him to be our mediator, unless he has from where he is one with the Father, and is one with us? This is shown very openly in the Gospel, already close to suffering, praying to the Father in such words: That they may be one, even as we are one. I in them, and you in me (John 17:22-23). Tell me, you who preach the one essence of Christ, how is he in us, and how is the Father in him? Because the substance of the Father and the Son is one. That is why he is also in us, because he wanted to become a partaker of our substance. There is therefore no longer one substance, but two: one in which He is one with the Father, the other in which He is one with us. one by which the Father is in him, the other by which he is truly in us; a true mediator, having whence he is nearest to God, whence he is nearest to us; that he may also make us nearer to God, certainly by himself he willed to be nearer to us. But if perhaps you, whom the consideration of the mediator impels unwillingly to the preaching of two substances, desiring to elude the force of truth, do not altogether deny the two essences of one mediator, but affirm that it was possible for these two to become one, inquire more carefully whether the Word and the flesh began to be of one nature, whether may the flesh and God the Father be preached of one essence. For consequently, since the Word of the Father is the Son, and undoubtedly the substance of the Father and the Son are one; as God the Father with his Word is of one substance, so with the flesh of his Word he will be found to be of one substance, if the flesh and the Word could become one substance.

7. Such an absurdity will also be added to this opinion, that since all human flesh is of the same substance, the flesh of Christ was human, which, according to you, began to be of one substance with the Word, and through the Word also with the Father; our flesh, and the divinity of the Father, are said to be of one nature: which no Christian ought at all to hear, or at least with a faint thought to receive to suspect. Whoever, therefore, asserts that there is one substance of Christ, thinks something else, which can easily appear to anyone, unless the eyes of his heart are obscured by the smoke of contention, by this preaching of one substance in Christ, the Father also was seen to be born of the virgin Mary, crucified under Pontius Pilate, and buried. For if there is no other nature than that of the flesh of the Virgin mother in order that it might be born temporarily, the only-begotten God received, but the assumed flesh and the assumed divinity became one nature in any way; Or will not this be one nature also of the Father, and how will homousion be predicated of the Father, as the Greeks say, of one substance or essence? or if he will be both of the Father, and begotten in himself, the Son crucified, let them see how the Father is said to be either unbegotten or impassive. Yes, not only the Father, but also the Holy Spirit (since he and the Father and the Son are believed to be of one substance or essence) will be associated with the passions of the Son; as if every dispensation of the Lord's incarnation will be thought to belong to the whole Trinity, and blessed Mary will not be the mother of the Son of God alone, but the mother of the whole Trinity. We rely on the apostolic examples to do this. The blessed Apostle speaks thus: Our old man was crucified at the same time, that the body of sin might be emptied (Rom. 6:6). How can our old man hang on the tree alone with Christ, except because he hangs on the tree according to that substance which he took from us? Also mentioned in another place, the Apostle says: And at the same time he was raised and made to sit in the heavenly places in Christ Jesus (Eph. 2:6). Let it be answered, how were we raised together, or are we seated together in the heavenly places, except through the communion of that substance which he took from us? If, then, the Son of God took the nature of his divine substance into unity, so that divinity and flesh might be one nature, what was united to his divinity was united to the whole Trinity: especially because the works of the Trinity are inseparable, because the

substance or essence of the Trinity is one. Now the Trinity is the Father, and the Son, and the Holy Spirit; three in persons, one in substance or essence. In which essence or substance, if the Son was born or suffered, the Father and the Holy Spirit were both born and suffered. But if the Son suffered so much, as the ancient tradition of the Catholic faith taught, he suffered in another nature. And what is other than human? If, then, there is one human nature and another divine nature, in Christ there is not one nature made of two.

8. The Arians are wont to object to us with such a proposition. They say that the divinity of the Son has passed, or it has not passed. If we answer: There was no suffering, they say: Therefore the pure man was crucified. If we answer, as we ought to answer: It has suffered, but according to the flesh, yet it is permanent in that which is impassive, they answer: Therefore either the divinity of the Father has suffered, if the divinity of the Son has suffered; or the divinity of the Father and the Son is not one. To the Arians who propose this, it is appropriate to answer in the Catholic language: The Father and the Son are one substance, not persons: the nature of the Father and the Son is one; but the person of the Father is different, that of the Son. But the Son taking flesh, that is, man's full and perfect nature, was thus designed to take it up, so that he might become one person of flesh and word, but not one nature. God, becoming man, united to himself the human nature, but in the unity of person which he does not have in common with the Father, not in the unity of substance which he has in common with the Father. Therefore, not the Trinity, but only the Son was both born and suffered. There is a different nature, according to which the Son suffered: but because he made the person of his divinity and flesh to be one, because of the unity of the person, the divinity of the Son is said to have suffered whatever the flesh brought forth. Now the person of the Son is not that which is the Father's, because it is different from the Father's: therefore only the Son suffered. But those who want to preach one nature, just as the one person of the Lord Jesus Christ, what will they answer to the Arians? All their arguments will doubtless fail; and either they will agree with the Arians, that they do not preach the one divinity of the Father and the Son; or they will be associated with the Patripassians, by the sacrilegious error of being miserably bound. Heretical fury returns to the most pious sense; and he who confesses that two natures have become one in the Lord Jesus Christ, let him tell me which of these has perished, that the two might become one.

The divine could not perish, the human should not have perished. Or if he dares to assert the destruction of any one, let him say whether the one has been exchanged for the other: and if he suspects that the one could have been exchanged for the other, let him say again whether the divinity was converted into flesh, or the divinity into flesh. For if the divinity is reduced to the lower quality of the flesh, it is recognized as deteriorated; and already the good creator procured misery for himself rather than mercy for us. But if the permanent and inviolable divinity absorbed the substance of the flesh, so that this flesh began to be the Word, who could tolerably hear that a creature which had previously received all accidents had reached the kind and power of the creator, so that it was suddenly without quality, without quantity, without time, without place, without situation. without passions, without habit, in the lost condition of doing, supported only by the vigor of doing?

9. I fear that the increase of the creature of the creator is rather a diminution, as if God needed to be increased by the addition of flesh; because that nature could be changed much more easily into which the other could be changed. Let us take a very absurd opinion in silence; and if it is clearly clear that neither of these two natures could be transferred into the other, let him answer whether it is possible that the mixture of the two natures, without the property of any of them being preserved, has made a new nature of a new kind. And if he wishes to preach this one nature of one mediator, I do not, meanwhile, require what natural name he deems to be called; as how out of two natures, soul and flesh, one nature was made, whose name is man; from two animals in like manner one animal is born, and is called a mule; from the two substances of fire and wood, one thing is made, and is called coal; nor the soul alone, nor the body, man; nor the horse alone, nor the ass, nor the mule; nor can fire alone, or wood, be called coal by its natural name; so it may be worth showing from the two natures, that is, divinity and humanity, if nature has become one, what ought to be called natural. For Christ is the name of office; Emmanuel is a name implying both substances which are joined together; but of nature the name of that substance which could have been made into one is said to be from two, I have neither read nor heard through the language of any debater. This name, as I have said, I am vehemently searching for. But rather I propose this, I oppose this thought to the preacher of the one substance in Christ, even if he does not want to: If the nature of Christ is one composed of two, not such is the nature of the Father,

not such is the Holy Spirit. How, then, will the Son be homoousion with the Father or the Holy Spirit? The one nature of the Father and the Holy Spirit is simple, it lacks composition; But Christ, whose works are established by two single natures, is composed and lacks simplicity. What then shall we say? It may be that the violence of the truth urges us not to preach the one nature of Christ; or of the Father, and of the Son, and of the Holy Spirit, that is to deny the one substance or essence of the Holy Trinity. But if we deny one substance or essence of the Trinity, we seem to give assent to the doctrine of the Arians. Let us not therefore be seen to be like the Arians, although we do not predict one nature of Christ from two, but rather confess one Christ from two and in two natures; Let us not be polluted by the poison of the Arians, nor be intoxicated by the superfluous debate of the delirious Eutyches. God the only begotten, the true and proper Son of God was one, when in the beginning there was the Word, and the Word was with God, and God was the Word. This was in the beginning with God. All things were made through him, and without him nothing was made (John 1:1-3). It is one and the same when the Word became flesh and dwelt among us. Therefore, before the Virgin Mary conceived, God created us as a Trinity; and after having given birth to Emmanuel by fertilizing the Holy Spirit, that is, God with us, God the Trinity redeems us: before the dispensation of the flesh, our God the Trinity; after the business of the cross, and after the spoils of hell, our God the Trinity. Why this? because as one was, is, and will be the Father, who was not born of a Virgin; just as there was one, is, and will be the Holy Spirit, who likewise was not born of the Virgin; so also the Son, who was born of the Virgin, is one. His assumption was that of another to one person.

10. Therefore, through the birth of the flesh in Christ, the number of substances increased, but the singularity of the person continued. Therefore, although the nature of divinity is different, that of humanity is different, that quaternity does not become the Trinity; because there is a Trinity of persons, which remained one in Christ. Hence Christ is one, and always one, because of the singularity of one person, which in him can neither be divided, nor subdivided, nor duplicated, although he is believed to be of two and in two natures. Let us freely, therefore, without any fear, confess the two natures of one Christ, namely, the divine and the human, the Word and the flesh, appearing in manifest distinctions. to be completely adapted without

separation. For if someone asks me: I and the Father are one (John 10:30), whether that voice was uttered according to divinity or according to humanity; I confidently answer: According to divinity, not according to humanity. And if someone asks again: The Father is greater than me (John 14:28), whether that word was uttered according to divinity or according to humanity; I confidently answer: According to humanity, not according to divinity: and yet for this reason none of them will be the voice of Christ; for each word pertains to one Christ, whose divinity and humanity are: no separation has been introduced here, because we have said that one word can be understood according to one substance, but we have denied it according to the other. For the voice of each nature is appropriate, therefore it is not appropriate to the other without separation, because it belongs to that person, whose nature is both. No one imposes on us the necessity of preaching one nature. The Catholic faith ignores the two sons, and absolutely abhors those who assert the four; and therefore now, as far as I think, to some who keep the rule of the right faith, it was agreed to confess one passage concerning the Trinity. For this sentence is known to insinuate nothing else, except that he himself suffered in the flesh, who was born of God the Father, that is, Christ, lest it should be thought that a pure man endured the injuries of passion. This, then, says he who says one thing about the Trinity. He is not the fourth person who suffered, but belongs to the number of the Trinity. For the Son of God, remaining impassible according to his divinity, became subject to passion by assuming a susceptible nature. And although there is another nature in him by which he always remains impassive, another by which he is said to have suffered temporarily, yet he himself suffered impassive: not another is impassive, and another has suffered. But this impassive one is the Son of God, the only-begotten God, born naturally from God the Father centuries ago; and of the mother, after the fullness of time had come, mercifully, because he willed, he was begotten: without whom the Trinity never existed; since, as we have already explained above. There is a Trinity, the Father, and the Son, and the Holy Spirit: and whether you take away the Father, or the Son, or the Holy Spirit, there cannot be a Trinity; neither the Father, nor the Son, nor the Holy Spirit are counted as creatures according to divinity; neither the Father, nor the Son according to divinity, nor the Holy Spirit are said to be of this world, or of creatures; but each other is counted as a Trinity, and each one of them, while he is said to be of the Trinity, is separated from the rest of the creatures.

11. For every thing is either God or a creature. If God is, he is not a creature; if he is a creature, he is not God. But God is a Trinity of one substance or essence; The creature is divided into many kinds of different substances. Who then is God, and properly, that is, truly God, is either the Father, or the Son, or the Holy Spirit. And because neither the Father alone, nor the Son alone, nor the Holy Spirit alone is the Trinity, but together the Father, the Son, and the Holy Spirit, and the Father is one of the Trinity, and the Son is one of the Trinity, and the Holy Spirit is one of the Trinity. What then does he say, whosoever says: One Son of the Trinity, except: Seek him not among creatures? Therefore, according to the divinity, the Son, because he is not a creature, but a creator, is one of the Trinity; and because he himself according to humanity was condescended to suffer, for this reason he is said to have suffered one of the Trinity. It is, therefore, as far as I conjecture, nay, rather as far as I believe, that one of the Trinity has suffered, such as it is to say: God has suffered. But just as anyone who preaches God's passion does not make the substance of the divinity susceptible, but the impassive divinity and the humanity which is subject to passion, he shows that there is one person, so when he preaches one passion of the Trinity, he commends the unity of the person in both natures: excluding the nefarious and treacherous doctrine of the Nestorian heresy, which introduces two sons . He therefore denies one passage of the Trinity, who wants to deny the passage of God. Now all the faithful understand well how God suffered, namely, according to the flesh, according to what God was able to do. Otherwise, there would remain no probable reason for the acceptance of the flesh, if the divinity could by itself be subject to passion. These things are so well known to almost all Christians, that whenever they hear it preached that God has suffered, they do not understand but the Son of God, nor do they think of suffering in any other way, except as God ought and could have suffered, according to the substance of the flesh which he received from his mother. Thus, whenever one of the Trinity is said to have suffered, no one is at least compelled to ask: Who is the one? Is it the Father? or the Son? or the Holy Spirit? But as soon as you say the passage, they immediately understand the Son, whom they only know the passage of those who contest the Gospels, watching in them also for this knowledge of correct preaching: so that although asserting one passage of the Trinity, I do not add, according to the flesh; yet it was rightly said to them, as if they felt that I had added this, if, however, the feeling of contention is driven away from a distance, they are more accustomed to attack than to believe all that they hear. I have been able to

discover nothing, after much thought, by which this opinion (which is asserted by some) can give favor to Eutychian. For the first lie of the delirious Eutyches was this: that the only-begotten God, when he was deigned to become man, did not assume flesh from the womb of a virgin; according to the truth: that there are now not two substances in Christ, divinity and humanity, but that one substance has been made of these two. Let us, therefore, carefully reconsider both these views, and let us inquire more carefully whether that view which admits of one passage concerning the Trinity can be joined to one of them.

12. What, I ask, can be done to deny the truth of the Son of God's maternal body, when one of the Trinity is said to have suffered? If he is one of the Trinity, is he not really the Son of God? and if he suffered, does he really have the truth of his mother's body? Otherwise, take away the body taken from the mother, and how could pure divinity suffer? Consider what is the flesh of Mary, without doubt susceptible and mortal: so that the flesh of the Word was susceptible and mortal, it has its origin from that flesh which was susceptible and mortal. Therefore, in the offspring, recognize the similarity of the species by the testimony of passion; and that the Eutychians were attacked rather than favored, when one of the Trinity is said to have suffered, whether you like it or not. Without a doubt, under these words even the preacher of one substance in Christ is refuted. For Christ to be one of the Trinity belongs to the divinity; to be believed to have suffered, for the sake of humanity. He who suffered would not be one of the Trinity unless he had one divinity with the Father and the Holy Spirit. He who is one of the Trinity would not suffer unless he had consubstantial humanity with his mother. Therefore let the preacher of one nature in Christ be silent. For he mentions two natures, who acknowledges one passage of the Trinity. He gnaws away at his suspicions in vain, who, while trying to understand what is well said, seeks to be slandered rather than to be taught. One passage concerning the Trinity is not undeservedly disliked by the Nestorians. For they wish to introduce a fourth person, to whom they consider the sufferings to have happened. Eutychians, however, does not agree with one passage about the Trinity, if it pleases him. For they evidently contend to deny that the two natures of Christ continue, which are clearly contradicted by this chapter: one substance is insinuated by the fact that he is one of the Trinity; other things are also insinuated by the fact that suffering is inferred. For the passion mentioned is evidence of a passive nature: a passive nature understood,

especially in him who is one of the Trinity, makes a clear distinction between two substances. But perhaps the listener, who is either too suspicious or completely slow, wants to be instructed in an open phrase: namely, that whenever we are pleased to confess either God has passed, or one of the Trinity has passed, because both God the Father and God the Holy Spirit, and at the same time the whole Trinity God; and the Father is one of the Trinity, and the Holy Spirit is one of the Trinity. But when we say that God suffered, let us immediately infer, according to the flesh, lest it be thought that either the whole Trinity suffered, or that the Son himself suffered in the substance of the divinity which he has in common with the Father. And in this part, indeed, it is to be done with such; and if they desire to hear in this way, it behooves us to speak in this way: One of the Trinity, that is, the Son, one person out of three persons, suffered according to the flesh which he took from us, that he might be worthy to endure suffering for us.

13. Let us add clear words so that we do not give occasion to a malicious interpretation, and think that we believe otherwise than we feel. It seems, however, to be admonished to whom the words simply arouse suspicion, that neither the divinity of Christ, nor the humanity, be denied as often as they are not uttered with the same tone of voice: There is one, says the Apostle, God the Father, from whom all things are; and one Lord Jesus Christ through whom are all things (1 Cor. 8:6). Behold, he said Christ the Lord, he kept silent about man, and yet it is not to be thought that he denied it. Again, writing to Timothy in another place: There is one mediator between God and men, the man Christ Jesus (1 Tim. 2:5). Behold, he said to man, God is silent; He did not, however, deny it (for so great is the ineffable virtue of the sacrament); and thus in one person the two natures were singularly and wonderfully united by God, who was mercifully made man, so that whether you say Christ Jesus or God, you also understand man at the same time. whether you confess man, you also understand God at the same time. In him divinity is human, and humanity is divine. For this reason he rather sows the suspicion of a certain separation or division, who does not understand two natures differently, unless he has heard both mentioned. Behold, we heard in the Gospel the voice of Christ saying: The Father is greater than me (John 14:28); which seems to have been said according to human nature: are we therefore to think that he does not have divinity in himself, according to which he said in another place: I and the

Father are one (John 10:30)? Didn't he ever say: The Father is greater than me, he kept silent, I and the Father are one? and when he said: I and the Father are one, he was silent, the Father is greater than me? But he denied none of these things. Let us therefore say to him, if it seems, that he is saying, The Father is greater than I; add, Lord, I and the Father are one; lest the Arians should not be considered equal. Many such things are met with by those who seek pious devotion. Behold, the Savior himself says again; I proceeded from the mouth of the Most High (Eccl. 24:5), which he spoke according to his divinity. Let us say to him, add, Lord: From the womb of a virgin, which pertains to humanity; lest the Manichaeans or the Eutychians think that you were not born of the flesh. Let us speak freely among those who know how we believe. The apostles were baptizing in the name of the Lord Jesus: was it because they were silent about the Father and the Holy Spirit that they were denying it? Or was that baptism not given in the name of the Father, and of the Son, and of the Holy Spirit, because the apostles are said to have baptized in the name of the Lord Jesus? Because of the communion of one substance, and because of the one name of the individual Trinity, even when the Lord Jesus alone is named, are not also the Father and the Holy Spirit known to have been named by virtue of that name, which is one of three? Even so, even if I mention only the divinity of Christ, I have already mentioned at the same time the humanity which he united to himself from the Virgin; and if I named humanity alone, I also named divinity, to which it is united. These two substances in Christ can be expressed without speaking to each other, they cannot be known without believing each other.

14. For behold, at Miletum, the blessed Paul was giving salutary warnings to the elders of the Church: Pay attention. he says, to you and to the whole flock, in which the Holy Spirit has appointed you bishops to rule the Church of God, which he acquired with his own blood (Acts 20:28). Just say, Doctor of the Gentiles, and answer us something, which even we, who are very suspicious, ought to answer. You said that God acquired the Church with his own blood; why did you not add the Son? What if another thinks the Father? What if another Holy Spirit? because the Father is without doubt God, and the Holy Spirit is God. Or if you simply named God, or when you said that he acquired the Church with his blood, you would say how God has blood, and you would add, according to the flesh: that no one should think that even divinity can have

or shed blood. I know how to answer this inquiry without delay. You know, O son, my preaching; Why did you doubt my opinion? I have already said: The Father did not spare his own Son, but delivered him up for us all (Rom. 8:32), so that the Son might be believed to have suffered so much from the Gentiles. I have already said: He who, being in the form of God, did not presumptuously think that he was equal to God, but emptied himself, taking the form of a servant, being made in the likeness of men, and found in the habit of a man. He humbled himself, becoming obedient unto death, and the death of the cross (Phil. 2:6-8), that he might be rightly believed to have died in the human body: but of whom, in order that you might know God, I spoke confidently elsewhere: Of whom Christ according to the flesh, who is above all things, blessed be God forever (Rom. 9:5). I know, Saint Paul, the most complete teaching of truth, and I have never had any doubts about your opinion in the book of the Acts of the Apostles. I understood that God, who acquired his Church with his blood (Acts 20:28), was none other than Christ Jesus, the Son of God, and that he had no blood except according to the substance of the flesh. But I said these things on account of those who, now hearing one passage about the Trinity, say: Add, according to the flesh; as if it should be understood otherwise, even though I will not add; or that it is necessary to add much, which, even if it is not added, is apparent. However, I willingly demand from myself that I suffer because I am ready to repay. The tongue brings forth uninhibitedly what the consciousness holds back. One of the Trinity, the Son of God, Christ Jesus, who is one person out of three persons, suffered according to the flesh. As for you, if you already believe that one passage about the Trinity is not maliciously said, say it in the same way with good sense as I do. But if you still doubt, say one person out of three who suffered, that is, the Son of God, the Lord Jesus Christ according to the flesh. and without any ambiguity possessed by the error of Judge Nestorius.

15. Therefore every Catholic should simply hear one passage about the Trinity, or simply say; or, speaking cautiously, yet not incredulously, let him admit that one person out of three has suffered; and therefore he judges no one a heretic, who says that one person of the Trinity has suffered in that sense, in which he also truthfully says that one person of the three has suffered; and together we will hasten to walk the way of the Lord, holding peace. Indeed, this is one of the Trinity, which is, one person out of three persons: because if you say, Christ is

one person, you are saying nothing else than, Christ is one. And if you say, The Father or the Holy Spirit is one, you say nothing else than that the person of the Father or the Holy Spirit is one. Indeed, one can also signify substance, but if you add the proper and manifest term of substance, as when you say, the Trinity is one, and immediately subsume it, God. Otherwise, take away the name which you add, where substance is signified, and say, if you dare: The Father, and the Son, and the Holy Spirit are one. For who does not at once understand, "They are one," in the second person, as a consequence, and rebuke the vanity of Sabellius? You see, then, that properly one belongs to the person to be signified, although by the term of any substance it can also signify a substance. So let us simply hear one passage about the Trinity, that is, one person out of three persons. And no one wants to oppose me: If we say one thing about the Trinity, let us say one thing about humanity, just as we say God, and again we say man. For when we say God, we also rightly say man, because both God and man are names of substances. But one, because it properly signifies a person; Let us by no means think of saying one and one, lest we appear to assert two persons. Therefore we clearly confess one thing about the Trinity, and not one thing about humanity; because God came to the womb of the Virgin, and by his coming bestowing on her the gift of fecundity without the taint of lust, powerfully and ineffably united human nature to himself, by such a bond of unity, that the person of the Word became the person of flesh, and henceforth the person of the Word and flesh was one. Therefore we can by no means say that one of the Trinity and one of humanity, or one of the Trinity and one of humanity, because in Christ Jesus humanity does not have its own separate person, but the person of the Word of God from whom it was received, itself became his own. We therefore distinguish the two natures of Christ in terms, in offices, not in persons. For this reason the apostle confidently says: But we preach Christ crucified, a stumbling block to the Jews indeed, but foolishness to the Gentiles; but to the Jews and Greeks themselves called Christ the power of God and the wisdom of God (1 Cor. 2, 23, 24). Behold, Christ crucified is the power of God and the wisdom of God. Why, then, is it not said that one of the Trinity suffered? Is not Christ the power of God and the wisdom of God one of the Trinity? But he who denies this must clearly say that even according to his divinity the Son is not one of the Trinity. But if, according to his divinity, Christ is one of the Trinity, and according to his divinity, God's power and wisdom are; But Christ crucified is the power and wisdom of God; It is certainly rightly said, because one of the Trinity suffered.

16. Nor should it move anyone, if this opinion, as is said by some, was really expressed by Eutychetis, the Apocrisian, in the Council of Chalcedon. Truth often speaks even through the ignorant. But our fathers, sitting in the council, did not consider the meaning of the speaker, not the words, and neither pronounced him Catholic because of this opinion, nor did they want to insert the Catholic opinion itself into the definitions, lest they should be seen to have approved the understanding of the speaker, rather than the words. However, the Holy Spirit wonderfully admonished the faithful afterwards, even by this sentence to rebuke the Eutychians, in which the prediction of natures is full of two, so as not to say: If Christ is one of the Trinity, and the Trinity is of one substance, but Christ is God and man; therefore of one substance. For Christ is one of the Trinity, and is God and man, and is not of one substance; lest the humanity which he assumed should be consubstantial with the Trinity; which sound doctrine condemns. I remember that at one time I understood a threefold reason which would compel some to doubt this opinion. The first, namely, lest, by a certain separation intervening, there should be one Trinity and another who is said to be one of the Trinity, just as the Father is one, the Son is another, when the Son is said to be of the Father; and another city, and another man who is said to be of the city. But even though the Father is the Father by having the Son, yet by the very name of the Father he shows that he is not the Son. And the city of men is a multitude, not a man: and therefore when it is said of the city that one is himself, another city is found. Now the Trinity is the Father, the Son, and the Holy Spirit; therefore you confidently say: The Son is one of the Trinity; nor can there be another Son, and another Trinity, because without the Son there is no Trinity. But the second cause of doubt seems to be, to those who are unwilling to say, one thing about the Trinity, lest the substance of the divinity should be seen to be susceptible. But this is impossible, and to the ears and minds of Catholics it always appears in such a way that it is suspected of malice rather than of caution: especially since while one of the Trinity is said to have suffered, and the Trinity has the meaning of persons, it is easy for anyone to see that because of the one person of the Word, who is impassible and of flesh who is susceptible, one of the Trinity has suffered to be pronounced But there is a third reason for doubt, lest to those

who say: One suffered from the Trinity, the most earnest investigator should say: What is one? and to those who answered: Son, let him say again: Therefore, if there is one Son of the Trinity, or one of the Trinity, the Trinity of sons is the Trinity, or the Son of the Trinity. To the answers: God, let him say: How can anyone be one God of the Trinity, since there is not one God, but the Trinity? But this doubt is easily met if we consider what the Trinity is. For the Trinity (which must often be said) is a Trinity of persons. What then is the Trinity but three persons? What are the three persons, if not the Father, the Son, and the Holy Spirit? In this Trinity, therefore, you find neither Fathers, nor three Sons, nor three Holy Spirits: and therefore you confidently say: One Son of the Trinity, because in the Trinity there is only one Son; signifying whose person we say one of the trinity, because he alone is rightly believed to have suffered, who, being truly and properly God, truly and properly became man, so that Mary may not be undeservedly believed to be truly and properly the blessed mother of God. For from the ever-virgin Mary, neither divinity could be born without humanity, nor humanity without divinity.

17. Anyone who esteems a future mother consubstantial with the divinity, if truly and properly Mary was the mother of God, fears disappointment; for indeed, since he who is born is always truly and properly consubstantial with the begetting one, God received from her the means by which he might become consubstantial with her, and thus he was designed to be born from her. So, therefore, properly, as truly, Mary gave birth to the divinity of the Son, but incarnate. For without flesh mortal man could not beget eternal divinity. What, then, did he properly beget? He manifestly conceived, by opposing signs and virtues, that God is born of man. What is it, he literally gave birth? She herself gives him the matter of the flesh according to which she is begotten, indeed by the working of the Holy Spirit, nevertheless from her own bowels, and therefore he also properly begat whom it was necessary to be born in this way: because she begat him in human nature, which she begat properly without any doubting. But whoever thinks or says that two substances could never have been generated from one substance, he says truthfully if he has heard that they were generated separately. Now, however, in that great and wonderful sacrament, which was manifested in the flesh, the divine substance was properly born according to the human substance; for it was not born separately, nor did divinity unite humanity properly born to itself: but by

uniting it to itself it was properly born. I will say still more plainly for the capture of my weakness, if God will remove the darkness of truth and falsity from the light of this discussion. The pure divinity was properly born from the Father, the same incarnate divinity was properly born from the mother. And this is the distance between the two generations of the one Son of God, because in the divine generation there was no humanity: in the human generation, the divinity that was properly born was united to humanity. For if I say, or wish to say, Mary, always a virgin, properly gave birth to humanity, and not properly to divinity, it will be seen that in some way she gave birth to a pure man, whom she in no way gave birth to in this way, because she properly gave birth to the Word made flesh. Rightly then, as far as I think, we say and confess: Mary is truly the mother of God Christ, so that there is no suspicion of fantasy. We also rightly confess that Mary is properly the mother of God Christ, so that by no means could a pure man, who by the merits of good works be afterwards raised to God, or by coming into himself the Son of God, begin to be called or become God, but that God conceived without beginning, from a certain beginning made man and is believed to have given birth. Another appropriate way can be found in which this sentence can be expressed without offense, if everyone says: Mary is properly the mother of God Christ, so that this singular benefit of the heavenly operation is not seen as common with the rest. For the Savior himself told them in the Gospel: Behold, thy mother and thy brethren stand without, seeking thee: who, saith he, is my mother, or who are my brethren? And extending his hand to the disciples, he said: Behold my mother and my brothers. And everyone who does the will of my Father who is in heaven, this is my brother and sister and mother (Matt. 12:47-50). Therefore everyone who does the will of his Father is his mother. But Mary is therefore properly a mother, because by being born of her he became her son according to the flesh. Many God-fearing women give birth to God Christ in the mind, not in the flesh: but Mary alone gave birth to God Christ also in the flesh; and therefore she alone is properly the mother of God, because there is no other such mother of God. The blessed apostle, while writing to the Romans, said: If God is for us, who is against us? He spared not even his own Son, but delivered him up for us all (Rom. 8:32). Let someone tell me, then, whether the proper Son of God the Father is the proper Son of the Virgin Mother, or perhaps Mary did not have her own son, as God has his own Son? But Mary also has her own son, because she gave birth, she did not adopt him: and he has his own son, whom God has his own Son, because the Catholic faith never preaches two sons. It remains, then, that if God is the proper Son of God, he is also the proper son of the Virgin mother, and he properly begat him. Otherwise, if she did not properly give birth, neither is he a proper son. But the son is more proper; therefore he begat her properly: but according to humanity, according to which God could be born.

18. It now remains, at the conclusion of this volume, to give a certain rule of faith, by which the preceding simplicity of the speakers may be manifested, and the scandal of the hearers be removed, with the same two sentences about which the brothers disputing among themselves make a long dispute, lest any ambiguity should remain or appear suspicious. Therefore, when he was about to say one passage about the Trinity, he first asserted that the omnipotent God has one substance, that there are three persons: of which one person, that is, the Son, the eternal God, became man, and was born and suffered; neither by the Father nor by the Holy Spirit incarnated alike, although the work of our redemption was done by the whole Trinity. And let him confess that the Son suffered in this way, so that the believer understands that he could not have suffered in the very substance in which God, and with the Father and the Holy Spirit, is one God, but in that which he received from his mother without the Father and the Holy Spirit. But therefore the divinity of the Son can rightly be said by the faithful to have suffered, because it is his flesh that suffered, and it belongs to his person, which is not believed to have in common with the Father and the Holy Spirit. But after God the Son of God had suffered, and had not been made to suffer in the divinity itself, but in the humanity which had been made to suffer, he understood the suffering; let it be confessed, nevertheless, that the one Son of God, the Lord Jesus Christ, has two natures, or substances. And when he had more fully emphasized these things as a measure of his character or speech, he professed to follow in all things the decrees of the Council of Chalcedon, and the letter of Pope Leo. Adding, that by the incarnation of the Son of God the Trinity did not grow, nor did a fourth person join the Trinity; because in Christ the very person remained uniquely of divinity and humanity; that Nestorius, in introducing two sons, denies that, having rightly replied to his followers in the language of a faithful Catholic, in order to remove the quaternity, he says one of the Trinity passed; which, however, he insinuates that according to divinity he is one of the Trinity, but according to humanity he is a passer. Therefore, when Christ is going to say one

thing about the Trinity, let him first say what we have said; especially when he speaks to those who contradict him or suspect him badly; and he does not edify another, who thinks that he is instructing such things in a bad sense. I do not want the preacher of the Word of God to be content only with the testimony of his conscience: he should try to bring to the hearts of others what he feels rightly and faithfully; neither laziness nor pride will be revoked, as if emphasizing a doubtful matter, until it is devoid of all ambiguity. Let him be verbose, as much as necessity compels him, so long as he does not offend anyone by his obscure brevity. In the same way, if he were to say that the blessed Mary truly and properly gave birth to God, having first confessed all that, the divinity of the Son of God already begotten of the Father, he could not have been born, nor properly begotten, unless he had taken on the flesh of our race and the rational substance of the soul, that is, a full man: neither the beginning to have been given to divinity by a temporal birth, but to the flesh, the beginning or conception of which was only the assumption of divinity. First let it also be confessed that neither the things of divinity can be separated from humanity, nor the things of humanity can be separated from the divinity of Christ; but whether that which is said, done, or tolerated according to divinity, or that which is said according to humanity, its substance is common to both. Because of one person (which he often does not hesitate to emphasize) whom the preacher of the right faith preaches; although he knows, according to humanity, that divinity was properly born from the womb of his mother, yet he confidently says: Mary gave birth to God properly; He begat him, who is thus believed to be a man, so that God is not denied. But he who hesitates to pronounce these sentences, if he has heard all that is usually under the heretical side refuted with clear and absolute words, let him be free from suspicions, leave aside the contentions, and from the rest, take one passage about the Trinity, or accept that Mary is properly the mother of God, as is said by the Catholics. Even if the heretics endeavor to assert otherwise, let the orthodox teachers lend a simple ear.

EPISTLE IV. TO THE EGYPTIAN PRIESTS. Of the essence of the Trinity, and of the two natures of Christ.

1. To the most blessed Lord, brother Eugippius, the presbyter Ferrandus the little, greeting in the Lord. My dear, consider what force the question proposed

by Count Arianus has recently. But first, let us consider what opinions or dogmas the Arians and the Catholics differ from each other. Arians want to preach an individual Trinity, just as the Scriptures preach one God. Catholics, on the other hand, soundly listening to the precepts of the law: Hear, O Israel, your God, God is one (Deut. 6:4), lest they be seen to exclude the faith of the Trinity under the religion of one God, by preaching three persons of one substance, they simply confess the Trinity itself, one God; and they understand what has been wisely said about the Holy Trinity: Hear, O Israel, your God is one God. The Arians preach three substances, the Father and the Son and the Holy Spirit, and therefore divide their power, avoid unity, diminish immensity, and through errors subject the lesser Son to the greater Father; and they call the Holy Spirit the lesser Son. Catholics, on the other hand, confess that God the Father, God the Son, and God the Holy Spirit, lest they seem to introduce three Gods to the nations, are one in honor, glory, greatness, eternity, divinity, equality, and essence; and desiring to put no one before the other, yet they feel that the Son was born of the Father, and that the Holy Spirit proceeds from the Father and the Son.

2. If you wish to ask the Arians whence the Son is, they are afraid to say, concerning the essence of the Father: lest the one divinity of begotten and begotten should be proved, and equality confirmed. They fear again to proclaim the Son born of nothing, lest the Creator, taking an origin similar to the creature, and deprived of the privilege of the only begotten, should lose the glory of the Creator. On the other hand, they are much more afraid of creating a Son born from another source, that is, from some subjacent matter; lest any thing should appear to have been before him, by whom all things were made. To such errors the Catholics answer: Believe that he was born of the essence of the Father: if you deny it, say whence he is. They also say that the Son is lesser, because they deny that he is equal. But the Catholics say that he is equal in divinity, but inferior in humanity. His equality according to divinity has no beginning; nevertheless, neither the equality proper to the divinity, nor the diminution proper to the flesh, has an end. If, therefore, he is said to be inferior according to the flesh, he is said to be equal according to the divinity, Christ is the same and one, truly the Son of God and truly the Son of man. For the equal, persevering, became the lesser: having become lesser, he remained the equal. And therefore he is wholly inferior, wholly equal: because both natures

are preserved in him, both that which he had and that which he assumed from his mother. In any case, if both person and nature existed in Christ, one Christ could not be said to be lesser and equal to one Father.

3. We also say of Christ that Christ is truly one. However, to wise minds, whenever they hear, Christ is one, it is appropriate to think how he is one; whether having one person, or one nature. If it cannot be said to have one nature, which we say has received another, it can still be said to have one person, since that person, always remaining in the nature of the always remaining, later voluntarily took on such a wonderful nature without a person, that having no human substance a subsisting and remaining person, receiving into its unity. he would make it belong to himself; and henceforth that divine humanity which had begun as God, from which it had begun to exist, would become to have a person: that human divinity, since it wanted to unite to itself a truly human nature in the unity of a person.

4. Therefore we say, Christ is one, God is one, and the Son of man is one; that is, the person of Christ's God and man is one; however, we do not say that the nature of Christ's God and man are one. Agreeing with the Apostle, wanting to prove the unity of the person: For in what, he says to the Corinthians, what I gave, if I gave anything, was for your sake in the person of Christ (2 Cor. 2, 10). Would it not be better to say persons, if he wanted to signify two substances in Christ? Employing the same evident difference of substances, he says in another place: Although he was crucified, he was crucified because of infirmity, but he lives by the power of God (2 Cor. 13:4). Is not he himself crucified who lives? And yet he who was crucified by infirmity lives by the power of God. Wherefore to the love and commendation of one person, one Christ is thus preached, that sometimes one of his human or divine nature may be remembered, and yet both may be understood: since there is unity, so that he who names one, signifies both. Because of this the Apostle touches humanity alone, saying to Timothy: There is one God, one mediator between God and men, the man Christ Jesus (1 Tim. 2:5). Concerning the divinity he says to the Corinthians: For although there are those who are called gods (indeed there are many), yet for us there is one God from whom all things are, and one Lord Jesus Christ through whom all things are (1 Cor. 8:5).--The rest is lacking.

EPISTLE V. TO THE SEVERE SCHOLARS OF CONSTANTINOPLE
That our Lord Jesus Christ is one of the holy and individual Trinity.

1. You try to attach to me the business of great men, because of those who deny that our God Jesus is one of the holy and individual Trinity, what I feel pleased to hear. But this, I confess, the smallness of my intellect is either scarcely worth, or dare not assume at all. For who am I, or what sort of self am I, to whom it is permitted to pronounce a settled opinion on doubtful matters, and to determine new discourses in the authority of election, whether they should be accepted in later times? May God grant me to be content with the simple faith which the Catholic Church throughout the whole world teaches, so that, if possible, spending all the miserable time of this life in prayer and fasting, I may lament with my little brothers the many grievous offenses that I have already committed. , or what I am still forced to commit from the weakness of the flesh! I will surely consider myself blessed then, when, sitting in the silence of the monastery, I will sing that verse of the psalm for a few moments: I said: I will guard my ways, that I do not transgress with my tongue (Ps. 38:1). Let them speak and preach to whom the honor of the priesthood gives authority to teach; we are ready to learn; We do not presume to teach others. Therefore, most prudent man, if you wish to hear anything of the truth, ask, first of all, the antithesis of the apostolic see, whose sound doctrine is established by the judgment of truth, and is supported by the defense of authority. Ask the many pontiffs in different parts of the world, to whom the knowledge of the heavenly teachers, divinely inspired, has gathered a great fame for themselves with veneration. These, without doubt, are both fit to debate, and ready to persuade by frequent practice, and you will not be blamed if you consult them still uncertain; and you are praised if you follow the truly learned. And so demand from me the debt of charity, so that you do not suggest incurring the guilt of rashness.

2. It is enough for me, because of the clear sentence of the blessed Peter, which speaks generally to all believers: Be prepared to answer everyone who asks you an account of the faith and hope that is in you (1 Pet. 3:15); To those who are wondering how we believe, we should immediately answer: We believe in one God, the Father, and the Son, and the Holy Spirit, the Father begotten of no one, the only-begotten Son of the Father, the Holy Spirit begotten of the Father

and the only-begotten Son ever proceeding; so that in this blessed Trinity, which we have called one God, the Father is not the Son or the Holy Spirit, the Son is never the Father or the Holy Spirit, the Holy Spirit is sometimes neither the Father nor the Son, but the Father alone is the Father of the Son, so that the Son alone is the Son of the Father. But the Holy Spirit of the Father and the Son is a common Spirit. At the same time, these three are naturally one God, because they are one God, having one substance; for the reason that the Father, and the Son, and the Holy Spirit, are three persons; on account of the fact that God is one, all working at the same time inseparably; for the reason that the Father, and the Son, and the Holy Spirit, claiming certain things as their own: as begetting of the Father alone, and begotten of the Son alone, and proceeding from both, we acknowledge the Holy Spirit alone. Just as the Father spoke from the cloud: This is my beloved Son, in whom I am well pleased (Matt. 3:17); The only Son born of the Virgin, and baptized by John in the river Jordan; and that the Holy Spirit descended only in the form of a dove. For once upon a time the truth refuted those heretics, who so wished to call one God the Trinity, that they imagined the Father whom they confessed to be the Son himself, the Holy Spirit himself; ; and again, at the consummated mystery of the human dispensation, coming upon the apostles in tongues of fire, the Holy Spirit would be called: by this error they were compelled to believe not the Son of God the Father, but the Father crucified. Hence antiquity shows that they were also called Patripassians. Thus, therefore, because of one substance, Sabellius refused to admit three persons, just as, on the contrary, Arius, because of three persons, wanted to preach three substances. Indeed, the Apostolic Church counting three persons against Sabellius, but claiming one substance or essence against Arius, remembers what was said to them: Hear, O Israel, the Lord your God, God is one (Deut. 6:4); so that this one God is not solitary, but a Trinity, that is, the Father, the Son, and the Holy Spirit. With this confession preferred, the great and wonderful sacrament of piety (1 Tim. 3:16), which was manifested in the flesh, was justified in the Spirit, appeared to angels, was preached among the Gentiles, was believed in the world, was taken up in glory, spreading subsequent veneration , so for the redemption of the human race we believe that he took on human nature so that he who was and continues to be the only begotten God in the perfect Trinity, would himself become the firstborn of many brothers from Mary (Rom. 8:29); and this same one whom God the Father had begotten before all times, man the mother should beget him, after the fullness of times had come.

3. For principally our faith preaches Christ the Son of God, the Son of man, so as to say that the Son of God and man is one; nor should one worship Christ in divinity, the other in humanity, but he who is in divinity, himself in humanity. For this is why God became man, because there is no other God and no other man; but absolutely who is God, man himself; and for this reason, who is man, is also God, Jesus Christ our Lord. For God the Son, remaining one person in the Trinity, came to the Virgin; nor did he assume another person from her, but he assumed another unity of his person, so that the person who had always assumed the nature of the flesh, and had two natures in one person of Christ. Nor is it necessary to wonder how it is believed that human nature, from its beginning, had the person of the Word of God; knowing that God did not assume a man formed, nor conceived, nor a life of his own, nor already beginning to live in his mother's womb; but absolutely before Mary had conceived anything, before all the cause of man being formed and formed, God willing to become man, lived within the virginal palace of the womb; and by the power of divinity, bestowing the gift of fecundity, he took from her whom he wished to have a mother, the true flesh of our race. And by the very assumption he was conceived and born, he certainly did not take on another person, because he did not find a ready man, but instead took on a human nature, in which God himself would be born as a man. Therefore, human nature, from which it was created, had a person; but one with God, who was created by receiving it. Therefore, whoever contradicts this faith, show me humanity in Christ without divinity, and then I will admit that he had his own person even by human nature alone. Because the divinity of the Word of God was indeed without humanity, and humanity was never without divinity; therefore the divine nature had a person, which, when it received the human nature, it indulged; so that both the receiving nature and the receiving nature, ineffably united without any confusion, might be believed to be one person; whereas whose divinity is, his is his humanity; and whose humanity is his divinity: and although the divine nature is one, the human nature is another, yet there is not one Christ, whose divine nature is, and another Christ, whose human nature; but let there be one Christ, whose nature is human and divine. For the Word of God did not dwell in Christ, as in the prophets, but the Word was made flesh, that He might dwell in us (John 1:14). This is the Lord Jesus Christ. In short, of no prophet, although they often speak from the person of God, the Holy Scriptures told that God was above all things. But the apostle confidently cries out about Christ: From whom is Christ according to the flesh,

who is above all God, blessed forever (Rom. 9:5). For if anyone denies that the Christ of God and the Son of Man have one person, he preaches two Christs; and if Christ is to be worshiped or worshiped double, he does not worship the Trinity, but the four. If any one again says that there is one nature of Christ, and although he does not dare to deny that he is of two substances, yet fears or doubts that he confesses in two substances, he has asserted either the abolition of one nature, or the confusion of both. For unless he takes away one of the two at the same time, or confounds both, he will not have one as he predicts.

4. Briefly refuting these with the evidence of the Scriptures, so that the mode of the epistle may be kept, let us first consider the words of our Savior, to whom he delivered the fixed rule of divine baptism, saying this to his apostles: Go, baptize all nations in the name of the Father, and of the Son, and of the Holy Spirit (Matt. 28, 19). For those who think that Christ does not have one person, I ask: When the Son is named in baptism, if there is not one person of God and man, what person is named? If they say, Sons of God, they do not confess that this is the son of man, who is the Son of God; therefore all is removed from the sacrament of regeneration by the grace of the mediator. For there is one, as the Apostle says, the mediator between God and men, the man Christ Jesus (1 Tim. 2:5). And if (which is absent) when the Son is named in baptism, only the person of the Son of God is named, and the person of the Son of God of man is not mentioned, the mediator is not named. And how is the Father reconciled without a mediator? or if by chance he is not reconciled, why should baptism be given? But if it is reconciled, it is reconciled through a mediator. If it is reconciled through a mediator, this mediator is not only God, nor only man, but God the man; that he may unite man, having in one and the same person divinity with God, humanity with men, and for this reason a mediator. For if there was one God, another man; that is, God Christ had another person, Christ the man another; nor is that person of Christ, who has divinity with God, our mediator, because he does not have humanity with us; nor is the person of the Son of Man, who has humanity with us, our mediator, because he does not have divinity with God. Accordingly, if when we are baptized, we name only that person who has divinity with God, and how are we reconciled without a mediator? It remains, therefore, that if we wish to name the Mediator in the name of the Son in baptism, we do not divide the Son himself; but that this is God, whom we confess to be a man, let us truly

confound the deniers of one person. Otherwise, how will it be true, because whoever is baptized into Christ, is baptized into his death (Rom. 6:3), if when we name the Son in baptism, we do not name the one person of God and man, but the only person of the Son of God without the person of the Son of man; When, if there really were two persons, should the person of the Son of Man have been commemorated in order to commemorate the death of Christ in which the apostle teaches us to be baptized? For Christ could die according to man. But if he tries to deny one person in Christ, lest he exclude the sacrament of incarnation from baptism, he had asserted that the person of the Son of man was named by the name of the Son; therefore we do not baptize in the united name of the Trinity. For the Trinity cannot be said, where God the Son of God is not named, if only the person of the Son of Man is emphasized.

5. So that the whole Trinity may be named in baptism, and the grace of the mediator may not be silenced, and the commemoration of Christ's death be renewed, it may be truly recognized that Christ has one person; as the Son is named in baptism, this is understood to be named as one person, of whom Paul also says the vessel of choice: For what I have given, if I have given anything for your sake, in the person of Christ (2 Cor. 2:10). This person, having all that is of God, having all that is of man, truly says what John the evangelist mentions: No one ascends into heaven, except he who descends from heaven, the Son of Man, who is in heaven (John 3:13). For how can no one ascend into heaven, except he who descends from heaven, if it is not one person of Christ who descends and ascends? If it is thought to have two persons, will it not doubtless be one person who receives, and another person who is received? one thing which is born of God the Father, another thing which is united to the Son of God, when he willed to be incarnated? And if it is so, the receiving person descends, so that the receiving person ascends; and it will already be false: No one ascends into heaven but he who descends from heaven. For the person of the Son of God descended and the person of man ascended, and so it is not that which descends that ascends. According to the perversity of the evil understanding of those who duplicate Christ, the necessity of disputing compelled him to speak. For the rest, therefore, no one truly ascends into heaven, except he who descends from heaven, because he is one person of the ascendant and the descender, according to the nature of divinity descending with compassion, according to the nature of humanity ascending with the

trophy of immortality. For the Teacher of the Gentiles, giving testimony to this matter, clearly states: He who descends is himself and he who ascends (Eph. 4:10): clearly he, not another; and if not another, one and the same inseparable person, of whom it is rightly said: No one ascends into heaven, but he who descends from heaven (John 3:13); and on account of which slow minds should be inculcated in the most right way, the Son of man who is in heaven. For here I ask: if there is not one person of God and man, how does he say: The Son of man who is in heaven, when did he yet speak in the world? How is it, I say, how is the son of man in heaven before the death of the cross, before the glory of the resurrection, before the triumph of the ascension, except because he clung to the unity of the person of the Son of God, who never departed from heaven; and therefore is the son of man in heaven, because there is always the Son of God who became the son of man? For it appears strange, strange, unless it is understood. The Lord says: No one ascends into heaven, except he who descends from heaven; and as if someone were asking: Who is this? He immediately answered without hesitation: Son of man who is in heaven. O Lord Jesus, in the beginning the Word, and the Word with God, and God the Word; Before you came down and became the Word flesh and dwelt among us, were you not only God, consubstantial with the Father and the Holy Spirit, and one person in the Trinity? How, then, do you now say: No one ascends into heaven, except he who descends from heaven; and do you immediately follow the person of the one descending, the Son of man who is in heaven? How did the son of man descend before you became the son of man, except that you who were from the beginning the Son of God, you God the only begotten, you who are one person in the Trinity, became the son of man; and thus became the son of man, so that your second person was not the other of the son of man?

6. Finally, this one thing is recommended when the Pharisees are asked by Christ: What do you think of Christ? whose son is he (Matt. 22:42)? And to those answering, David, Jesus says: How then does David call him Lord in the spirit, saying: The Lord said to my Lord, Sit at my right hand, until I make your enemies your footstool (Ps. 90:1)? For David calls him Lord, and how is his son? Where the Pharisees were indeed convicted and humiliated; but still we, if we seek piously, are warned. For why is the son of David the Lord David, except because the Lord David himself became the son of David? For surely if

Christ were not one person, he could not be the son of David, the Lord David. But that is why the son of David is the Lord David, because the person that the Lord David has is the same person that the son of David has. This one person, asking Philip and saying: Lord, show us the Father, and it is enough for us; He said, I have been with you so long, and have you not known me? Philip, who sees me, sees the Father also. How do you say, Show us the Father (John 14, 8, 9)? For when Philip saw with his carnal eyes only the man who was speaking, he heard it said to him by the man's mouth: He who sees me sees the Father also. Why this, except because man himself is God, whom he who sees sees also the Father? Otherwise, if there were not one person of God and man, he would not say, He who sees me; already seen in the flesh, still desiring to be seen in the divinity, but would rather say, He who sees my God sees the person of my God. But what is it to say to one who sees himself, Who sees me, but to say: I am he who is seen, I who am not seen? And he who already sees me outside carnally, if he sees inside spiritually, not another, but me; surely he who thus sees me sees the Father also. And immediately followed: I in the Father, and the Father in me. When would mortal flesh say, I am in the Father, and the Father in me, unless he himself, because of the unity of his person, was the immortal God, who had been crucified as a mortal man? Hear that he is still one, alleging the truth of the person in many ways. When he asked his disciples: Whom do men say that I am the son of man (Matt. 16:13)? After the many and varied opinions of men, some of whom believed that Elijah, some Jeremiah, some John the Baptist, some one of the prophets, was the Christ of God, the Lord of the prophets, the Lord desiring to distinguish himself from his servants, and desiring to impress upon those who saw him the one Christ: But you, said he, is it I)? Peter answered: You are the Christ, the Son of the living God. Here, if the Son of God and the Son of man had not been one person, how could the blessed Peter, calling himself Christ the Son of Man, as if contradicting himself, add: You are the Christ, the Son of the living God? Christ says, "I am the son of man." Peter says, "You are the Son of the living God." If there is not one person of Christ, Peter is asked about something else, he confesses something else. It is asked, Whom do men say that I am the son of man? and he answers: You are the Christ, the Son of the living God. But if the blessed Peter would never have deserved to be praised by the teacher's speech, unless he had confessed himself about whom he was questioned, from whom he had said to him, You, from whom he had heard, Me, He is the son of man, who is the Son of the living God. Of whom Paul, writing to the Hebrews, in order to always show him as one person, says thus: Jesus Christ yesterday and today, he is the same forever (Heb. 13:8). When he himself said what he once said, he also wanted it to be understood three times, as if he were saying: Jesus Christ himself yesterday, himself today, himself and forever: yesterday, before he took flesh; today, when, according to the prophecy of the prophet Jeremiah, This is our God, and no other will be esteemed besides him: who found every way of knowledge, and gave it to Jacob his child, and Israel to his beloved. After this he was seen on earth, and conversed with men (Bar. 3, 36, 38). Either when he sits at the right hand of the Father forever, or when he will come to judge the living and the dead (as the whole Church confesses in a symbol), always he, never another.

7. For by taking on the flesh, he united the natures, and did not duplicate the person. He united the natures perfectly, which are permanent without confusion, and which will last forever. For he united in such a way that neither divinity changed into humanity, nor humanity was absorbed by divinity, but both natures, kept safe, used their offices, were recognized by their works, and were called by their names, but were not distinguished by their proper persons. For the two substances, that is, the divine and the human, were not united in such a way as to become one substance; but that he should be of one person, and that Christ should always exist as one of them. For it is impossible that, while truth compels us to preach one person, we should dare to deny two natures. For if the Creator became a creature, if the Word became flesh, if God was found in habit as man; neither could the creator be created, nor the Word became flesh, nor could God be man without assuming another nature. And if second nature is assumed, there are certainly two natures, not one. But if it is asserted that one was made from two, it must first be said which was made. For although it is scarcely possible to make one thing out of two substances without the confusion of both, or the abolition of one, yet every time something is made from two into one, a new thing is made; and if a new thing is made, it necessarily takes on a new name of nature by existing anew. For example, in us there is one nature of the soul, another of the body: the spiritual, the earthly; the former invisible, the latter visible. And because from these two nature was made one, a new name for nature was acquired, to be called man. For the soul is spoken of separately, and the body separately; neither soul can be called body, nor body can be called soul, but at the same time body and soul are rightly called man. Neither is the nature of the soul the nature of the body, nor is the

nature of the body the nature of the soul; but at the same time consisting of the nature of the body and the soul, the human nature is one. Accordingly, if the divine nature and the human nature are affirmed to have made one nature, let it also be found which nature is neither divine nor human; but as new, so called by a new name. In this article of the proposition, no one who plainly rejects, and a contentious asserter of one nature, assigns a new name to the nature which he imagines to be one of two, and answers it to be called Christ; because Christ is the name of office, not of nature. For Christ is from the anointing; but the anointing seems to be a term of temporal dispensation, not of substance. For he who believes that one is made of two (I often say), let him say that one is. For this is one, and cannot be called divine, nor human, but by any other name: which name, if any one finds it, the asserter of one nature will be tolerable. However, I am very afraid to confidently assume the profession of one nature, because if the nature of Christ is one, either the whole will be equal to the Father, or the whole will be inferior to the Father. If all are equal, according to which he says: The Father is greater than me (John 16:28)? if the whole is less than he says: I and the Father are one (John 10:30)? Either impassive, or susceptible. If impassive, how is it said that Christ suffered, died, and was crucified? if he is passable, or Christ will no longer have one nature with the Father, so that God the Father may be separated from his passions; or if this one nature, which he has in common with the Father, will be susceptible, the Father will also be susceptible, and the Patripassians will no longer be Catholic Christians, but heretics will boast. I add further: if the nature of Christ is one, it is either asserted to be invisible or visible; if invisible, what did those who were crucified see? What did the apostles see until they were touched? What did the angels promise to see, saying: So shall he come, as ye saw him going into heaven (Acts 1:11)? But if he is visible, what did he want to reveal to his lover in the future, when he said: And I will love him, and I will manifest myself to him (John 14:21), already manifested according to the flesh? Or why does the Gospel so cry: No one knows the Son but the Father (Matt. 11:27)? For without doubt we know what we see; and no one can say that he is not subject to the notion which he has confessed to be subject to the vision.

8. It is still moving, because if the nature of Christ is one, it is either diffused everywhere or local: if it is diffused everywhere, why do we recite the words of the symbol like this: On the third day he rose from the dead, ascended into

heaven, sits at the right hand of the Father? Who will answer me, if the nature of Christ is everywhere diffused, how did he ascend into the heavens? if it is spread everywhere, how is it specifically said of it: He sits at the right hand of the Father? But if it is local, certainly the wisdom of God, which is Christ (1 Cor. 1:24), reaches from end to end with strength, and arranges everything gently (Wis. 8, 1). And where is it that when he withdrew from his disciples according to the presence of the flesh, he said, "Behold, I am with you until the end of the age" (Matt. 18:1)? Let us therefore be ashamed to deny two natures, that in one Christ it may appear which nature is equal to the Father, and which is inferior to the Father; what is susceptible, what is imperceptible; what is visible, what is invisible; which is diffused everywhere, and which is local; while yet Christ is one, both equal and lesser, both impassible and susceptible, both invisible and visible, and everywhere diffused and local: all equal, not all equal? all minor, not all minor; all invisible, imperceptible, diffused everywhere, but not all. But here, if you ask, what is the whole of Christ? I answer: The word of God, rational soul and flesh. For whether you speak the Word, Christ is whole, but not whole, unless you employ the rational soul and body. Whether you say the rational soul, Christ is whole, but not whole, unless you apply the Word and the flesh. Whether you say flesh, Christ is whole, but not whole, unless you apply the Word and the rational soul. Therefore the whole of Christ is everywhere according to the Word, but not the whole is everywhere; because there is not everywhere a rational soul and flesh, with which the whole is. The whole of Christ was in hell according to the rational soul, but not the whole, because the flesh was not there, with which the whole is. The whole of Christ was in the sepulcher, according to the flesh, but not the whole, because the rational soul was not there, with which it is whole: yet the Word of God was with his soul in the underworld, and with his flesh in the sepulcher, because it was naturally diffused everywhere, and neither of his soul nor was he ever lacking in his flesh. Therefore, whether the Word, or the rational soul, or the flesh is signified, the whole Christ is signified, but not the whole. For it will not be whole unless the Word, the rational soul, and the flesh are at the same time. But why is the Word the whole Christ, and the rational soul the whole Christ, and the flesh the whole Christ, except because it is one person of the Word, the rational soul, and the flesh? Wherefore again the Word without the rational soul and the flesh is not the whole of Christ; Or is the rational soul and the flesh without the Word not the whole of Christ, except because the nature of the Word is different, the rational soul and the flesh are different? that divine, that human? that simple, that compound? yet when the very person of Christ, which seems to unite two substances, divine and human, that is, simple and compound, is not compound, but simple in each, and simple in both; and so simple as it was before it assumed human nature in its unity; so that henceforth he had two substances, one (as we have said) simple, and the other compound.

9. But why do we dwell on more? This is my faith concerning the incarnation of Christ, by which I confess that Christ is one person out of two and in two substances. Nor does it matter how he could have two natures in the one person of Christ, when we see that the one substance of the Godhead has three persons. For if someone says to me: Show me in Christ according to the number of natures, the number of persons; I will answer fearlessly: Show me also you in the deity according to the number of persons, the number of natures. For if nature cannot exist without a person, neither can a person exist without a nature. But if in the Trinity it is said that all three persons have one nature, because that is the one nature of all three persons: so I will say in Christ that both natures have one person, because that signifying the existence of each is what distinguishes one from another. Wherefore it would be seen that the preacher of the two persons in Christ would rise up properly, if that God had not been man, or that man had not been God, a person distinguishing one from another; He would separate him from another who was to be believed in humanity. Nevertheless, this is far from the minds of the faithful, let it be far from Christian discussions. Accordingly, those who deny that our Lord Jesus Christ is one of the holy and individual Trinity, if they confess that our Lord Jesus Christ is God, the Son of God, made the Son of man; and therefore, when the Lord Jesus Christ is named, not a pure man, but a divine and human substance at the same time; if they confess that God is a Trinity, the Father, and the Son, and the Holy Spirit; and this Son without whom the Trinity never existed, and by whom the Trinity remained by assuming flesh; as the Trinity is always, from the beginning of his incarnation, they understand the Lord Jesus Christ to be himself: what about us, if they preach the right faith with any words? Rather, I think, it should be seen and considered more carefully why the Lord Jesus Christ is one of the holy and individual Trinity is too cautiously denied by some. For in three ways, as far as my opinion goes, the proposition of this opinion is rendered suspect. The first way is, lest the Lord Jesus Christ should therefore be thought to be preached to be one of the holy and individual

Trinity, so that another Himself, another Trinity of which it is said to be one, should be insisted upon. in which is the Son; or when, for example, of that city, or whether we indicate that someone is there; in so far he is another, another city; that without him the city may remain as it was with him, although he alone cannot be called a city. This sense, however, is more beneficial to those who wish to suppose the fourth person of the Trinity.

10. There is a second way. Perhaps the Lord Jesus Christ is fraudulently intimated to be one of the holy and individual Trinity; for this reason, namely, that not his humanity, which the Lord Jesus Christ began to be called by accepting into the unity of his person, but his divinity, because of which he is said to be one of the holy and individual Trinity, is said to be susceptible whenever the Lord Jesus suffered for the salvation of men is not silent. This sense, however, either helps the Arians to deteriorate the divinity of the Son, or it interferes with the belief that there is only one nature in him, while he fears to incur the suspicion of two persons. There is still a third way, lest, after affirming to us that the Lord Jesus Christ is one of the holy and individual Trinity, we should at once ask, What is one? For the example of a word, if I choose to say, Gabriel is one of the angels of God, when asked, What one? I answer, Angel, because I have already mentioned all those angels. Or if I speak again in the same way, that the Church of Ephesus is one of the seven Churches to which John the Apostle writes, when asked, What is one? I will soon answer, the Church, because I have already mentioned those seven churches. In the same way, if three men approached someone, or withdrew from someone else, I would say, when I say, One of these came to me, being asked, What one? I soon answer, Man, because I said those three men. But since we have said that the Lord Jesus Christ is one of the holy and individual Trinity, when asked, What is one? we cannot say, one God, because that Trinity is not of the Gods; nor does reason permit us to say: The Lord Jesus Christ is one God of the holy and individual Trinity; but rather we say: The whole Trinity is one God. Similarly, when asked, What is one? when we say that the Lord Jesus Christ is one of the holy and individual Trinity, we cannot answer, Son, because that Trinity is not of children; for the Son is one in the Trinity. And if it is said to say thus: The Lord Jesus Christ is one of the holy and individual Trinity, as if it were said, one person, this is said most correctly; but in a way that is convenient, if this seems so, one person is spoken of as one, so as not to cause offense to those of little

understanding, or to those who are ill-suspected. In what ways, therefore, this opinion is judged by some to be refuted or to be avoided, I have simply said: moreover, I neither contradicted those who wanted nor those who were unwilling to say: because nothing can be determined by me with certainty, I have already foretold in the beginning of this letter.

11. For the rest, if he sent us a certain opinion (which I therefore doubt to confirm, because I do not in vain think of anything intimated by your letters from it), I wonder how those who deny that our Lord Jesus Christ is one of the holy and individual Trinity, are said to confess him to be one of the holy and the individuals of the Trinity. I would like to hear what the difference between these propositions is proposed; if it were permitted, I would ask those present: I would like to say, if it were given, to insert the discourse without the desire of contention. For if the Lord Jesus Christ is to be said to be one of the Trinity, it must certainly be said because of the unity of the person, in order to show that the only-begotten God himself became man. Why, then, is it not also said of the Trinity, that it may be shown that it likewise belongs to the essence of the Trinity, because, assuming the form of a servant, it endured the insult of death? But if in that sense it is not said that he is one of the holy and individual Trinity, but that the Lord Jesus Christ is from the holy Trinity, that it may be shown that he has nothing in common with the Trinity in substance; substance (for everything that is from someone must also be from the same someone; however, not everything that will be from someone can immediately also be from the same someone: just as everything is from God, yet not from God; but the only begotten Son, and from We confess to God and from God most correctly); Your prudence also sees that the Lord Jesus Christ is preached by these as a pure man. and altogether this sense, unless perhaps better or more aptly explained, is to be judged most dangerous. Wherefore I think that we should desist from contentions, but rather wait persuasively, and patiently bear this doubt, until the universal authority of the Church either pronounces to be accepted, or betrays to be rejected. For true faith will not be preached any less if we are silent about this sentence; or unless it is strengthened by this opinion, it will be considered less firm: since, even if it were so, it would be more appropriate for us to follow the apostolic words, where it is said to us: Nevertheless, what we have arrived at, let us walk in it; and, If you mind otherwise, God will reveal this also to you (Phil. 3:15-16). We have arrived at

this, to know that the Lord Jesus Christ is of two and in two substances or natures, that he has one person. Let us hold this, let us know this, let us predict this; and if we utter certain words less cautiously, or if we are more anxious to keep silent, as if we knew otherwise, God will reveal this also to us.

EPISTLE VI. To Pelagius and Anatolius, Deacons of the City of Rome.

For the epistle of Iba, bishop of Edessa, and thus for the three chapters of the council of Chalcedon: against Acephalus.

1. Venerably following the most blessed and devout lords, the holy brothers and condeacons, Pelagius and Anatolius Ferrandus the Little. I suffered very great distress when we received your writings, the sign of which was a long silence. For if you deign to consider how hasty I am always accustomed to obey your orders, you will not delay this reply to the deputation of the less devotion. For why should I be silent for a long time, if I were not alarmed, not to tell the truth about the question that has recently arisen, to the silent but still African Churches, to speak before the time? Simply, however, by your compelling judgment, we speak what we believe, so that you may deign to know that we are with you in heart, with you in faith, with you according to good hope, with you in charity that is not false. For whatever things are intimated wisely, briefly, truthfully, we believe the same, feel the same, speak the same.

2. With the apostolic words I exhort the glorious ministers of the apostolic see: Stand, and keep the traditions which you have learned (2 Thess. 2:14). It is not expedient for the ancient Fathers, who are known to have been present at the council of Chalcedon, to censure the deliberation, to retract the judgment, to change the opinion: lest the venerable synod, established for so many years without any doubt among all the Churches of the East and West, should suddenly lose its reverence; nor can he maintain inflexible strength in the definitions of faith, if he begins in some part to be convinced of being weak or worthy of criticism. Whatever is once established in the council and congregation of the holy Fathers must always obtain perpetual firmness. For on this front we will sing: How much we have heard and known, and our fathers told us (Ps. 77:3); if I please, may I rescind their decrees as often as I please? Through those wisest judges the Catholic Church said that the Catholic

Church should keep, or rather that it has kept until now: why do we now again in today's debates reject an epistle that was not at all rejected then? The source is sealed, the Catholic Church; But James the Apostle cries out: Does a spring issue sweet and bitter water from the same hole (James 3:11)? If sweet water flowed to bring forth the definitions of the faith from the mouth of the ancient priests, how could it be that from their mouths, and not from others, as if from their hole, in the business of the venerable bishop of Iba, flowed not sweet water, but more bitter gall? I speak with fear and trembling, but still I say: If then the laudable discussion of the Council of Chalcedon has given the faithful a bitter taste in any business, let us give hands to the heretics, so that they may be permitted to accuse them of the salutary antidote as if it were a deadly potion, giving us the opportunity, "while the battle is in words, while there is a question about novelties, while there is an opportunity for doubts, while there is a complaint about the ears, while there is a struggle about studies, while there is a difficulty about consent. Your Beatitude knows more fully that these words, not mine, but those of the blessed Hilary, are contained in the second book which he writes to the emperor Constantius. Therefore, brothers, look out among the rocks among which the ship of evangelical preaching will float. Isaiah cries out: Woe to those who put darkness for light (Isa. 5:20); and dare we assert that our fathers said that darkness is light, when they refused to condemn the letter favoring Nestorius, nay, they even wished to accept it? Will the prophetic curse be attached to our fathers: Woe to those who put darkness to light? Were they not like lights in the world, containing the word of life, whose faith imposed silence on the unfaithful? In which true believers did the whole world believe?

3. Or is it said: They believed well, but the venerable Ibae received the letter badly? Were they truthful in their confession, but did they give unwary consent to the deceitful confession? Who shall bear the tortuous strife of useless questions? If any part is displeased at the Council of Chalcedon, at the risk of displeasing the whole. The most holy vessel of choice Paul clearly declares: A little leaven corrupts the whole mass (1 Cor. 5:6). If an acid mixture can be found in that mass of holy definitions, or of a little leaven, the whole mass will be judged harmful; or at least, to make a great exaggeration, useless for making the bread which strengthens the heart of man. What, then, did it profit that there Nestorius, there Eutyches, were anathematized? Behold, the condemners

of Nestorius and Eutyches are blamed for having received a letter favoring Nestorius with blasphemies, either ambiguous or manifest. What of course? If they admitted it ignorantly, they will be seen to have incurred the mark of ignorance, which is absent, so that their authority is completely emptied; but resisting their dogmas, they will cry out with much more insult: Behold, the synod assembled at Chalcedon, the great weight of authority without the slightest doubt, at one and the same time condemned Nestorius, and recalled the error of Nestorius, receiving a letter completely contrary to the Catholic faith; as you have just begun to feel, understanding, however late, how unwilling all those bishops were to understand the truth. Let us weep and pray, that such an error may soon be abolished, that it may disappear, that it may be rejected, and that it may be buried in perpetual silence. The whole council of Chalcedon, since it is the whole council of Chalcedon, is true: no part of it has any censure; We know that whatever was said, done, judged, and established there, was wrought by the ineffable and secret power of the Holy Spirit. Why do we slander the memory of so many righteous people with sudden contradictions, when Solomon, full of the Holy Spirit, will clearly say: The memory of the righteous with praise (Prov. 10:7)?

4. What if religious men, coming from their graves, before God before whom they live, with whom they faithfully rest, should say in the last resurrection: Why did you reject the letter, whose wording we felt was Catholic, we said, we judged, and we confirmed our judgment by signing it? Or because the venerable Ibas reproached Saint Cyril, the pontiff of the Church of Alexandria? But afterwards he declared that he had communicated the same to St. Cyril. If he deserved blame for the reproach of blessed Cyril, he deserved not the least grace for the restored communion. To blame the chapters of St. Cyril because of the ambiguity and obscurity of the expression, with the Eastern bishops having little understanding, was human weakness: so that he believed his words more easily and most willingly agreed with those who interpreted them well, he had been completely priestly of charity, without any loss of truth. Why should we condemn the epistle, where, as if it were past, both are narrated by the faithful interpretations of that holy Cyril? He himself, Saint Cyril himself, hastened to remove the scandal of bad intelligence, not from the venerable Iba, but from several Eastern bishops, by interpreting his chapters well: and we, for his insults, should we reject the epistle explaining what had happened to

history? If it is confirmed that the venerable Bishop Ibas spoke contrary to the rules of the true faith in that letter, because of certain or ambiguous or obscure things which make this appear, our opinion must be better, because we were able to investigate the meaning of the words from the mouth of him who dictated the letter. Lastly, why should we think that the letter favors Nestorius, the author of which, in the presence of us, commanding, and listening, did not at all hesitate to anathematize Nestorius, accepting the tome of Pope Leo, and confirming the confession of the true faith by signing with us? Hearing this, what kind of answer are we going to give to so many famous leaders and teachers of the Churches? Especially when the king is just sitting on the throne?

5. Let us beware, brethren, of the wiles of the devil. If in this letter of the venerable bishop of Iba, which the Fathers received, the nefarious error of Nestorius is thought to be on the side, it does not harm either the great or the small: for the error of Nestorius was publicly condemned in the Council of Chalcedon. If the reproach of the most holy memory of Cyril moves a scandal, so that the letter which the Fathers received is thrown away, he is praised there, and much praised; when his interpretation of his own sayings is confirmed to have removed the offense of the left suspicion, when his peace was reconciled with the Eastern bishops: in which peace all those who communicated with him slept together, and they said that this epistle referring to such things was not to be lightly blamed. By virtue of the religious emperor Marcian being present at the time, all the priests who had begun the council of peace with peaceful minds and ended it with the definitions of ecclesiastical peace, returned in fraternal peace to the places of their peoples, without hatred, without envy, without strife, in harmony, of one mind, bearing a common witness. There was the apostolic see among his legates, holding the primacy of the universal Church; there the pontiffs of other venerable seats, cunning as serpents, simple as doves; there was a great crowd of shepherds from the smaller states, governing the flocks of their flocks with pastoral concern. No one there condemned anyone against the will of others, no one acquitted anyone against the will of others; all agreeing with themselves, and willingly fulfilling the words of the Teacher of the Gentiles, obeyed him who said to them: I beseech you, brethren, that you all say the same thing, and that there be no schisms among you (1 Cor. 1:10). Therefore their judgment remained, and remained in its stability in no way altered, because the dignity of the judging priests was neither

inferior, nor small in number, nor less in authority, nor ignoble election, nor superfluous presumption, nor unwise deliberation, nor popular consent, nor fruitless labor, nor the opposite end to the tranquility of the Churches. They came to calm past conflicts, cut off present ones, and even mitigate future ones: to add something after their definitions, to change them, to reduce them, is nothing else than to sow new discord. No one is in a hurry to blame those who are well laid [Or arranged], no one to correct what is right. What will be firm, if what the Council of Chalcedon established is called into question?

6. I could lament more here with mournful complaints under a certain tragedy; but it seems to me to be sufficient what the Church of Justinian of Carthage, through the language of his glorious pontiff Capreoli of blessed memory, who wrote to the most clement prince Theodosius, reasonably defined, saying: "Nothing in divine and human acts, nothing in sacred as well as in public affairs, can obtain any firmness, if it which are closed due to the end of the judicial sentence, after the space of years and every volume of the centuries, as if in the amendment of the Fathers, as an instructor, posterity presumes to amend. And in another letter to the council of Ephesus addressed to the deacons by Versula: "Anything that may have recently arisen needs to be discussed, so that it can either be accepted as approved or rejected as condemned." On the other hand, those about which it has already been judged before, if anyone admits that he is called to recantation, it will be seen that he doubts the faith which he has held until now. Behold, no longer established only by synodals, but by judgments almost confirmed by the councils, the memorable doctor of the Carthaginian Church confesses that it is too guilty to be called again for an examination; How, then, will those who were once judged be judged now? If at that time any accuser of a letter whose dictation was known to be Catholic should challenge the greater courts, perhaps according to custom there would be room for an appeal; but where would he go? or where would he find elders in the Church to judge? having before him the apostolic see in his ambassadors, by which agreement, whatever that synod determined, he received invincible strength? The voice, then, taken away from those who wish to defend it was taken ill, how shall it be restored again? After so many and such pontiffs, who will be a new and competent connoisseur of the business already accomplished? From what parts of the world or states will the bishops better than the ancient bishops be gathered, to whom the power is

given to amend the opinions of the elders? or with what hope do they confidently assume to define something, seeing that the judgments of such men are suddenly overturned? How will it be possible for our successors to please what we are doing, if through us they will be taught to undo what they know their predecessors to have done? Whence this new caution? After Pope Leo, Anatolius, Maximus, Juvenalus, or the other priests of that time, was there not one of their successors who read more attentively and understood that the letter of the venerable bishop of Iba was badly inserted into the synod? The complaints of the heretics just began to move the Catholics to think of rejecting this letter.

7. I have to say: if the decrees of the Council of Chalcedon are revised, let us think of the Synod of Nicaea, lest we suffer a similar danger. The universal councils, especially those to which the consent of the Roman Church came, hold the place of second authority after the canonical books. Just as the readers of divinely inspired Scripture are not allowed to criticize anything, even though they are by no means capable of comprehending the depth of the heavenly oracle, but the pious reader also believes what he does not understand, so that he deserves to understand what he believes. Thus, in no other way, do the councils which the ancients established and preserved, demand obedience from us, leaving no need for doubt. They are far from those of which the Apostle says: Prove all things; hold that which is good; Abstain yourselves from every form of evil (1 Thess. 5:21-22). But those things which are concluded by the judging of the holy bishops, and brought to the memory of the blessed are more carefully examined and confirmed, are to be followed, are to be embraced. especially among the posterity, those already dead according to the flesh who brought forth the judgment, and already established there where, according to the Gospel, the Father judges no one, but has given all judgment to the Son (John 5:22). What good is it to have a struggle with those who sleep, or to disturb the Church on behalf of those who sleep? If any one, accused and condemned while still in the body of this death, before he deserves to be acquitted, is taken from the world, he cannot be acquitted further by human judgment. If someone who has been accused and acquitted in the peace of the Church has gone over to the Lord, he cannot be condemned by human judgment. If someone accused before the day of the priestly examination is prevented by a sudden call, placed within the bosom of the mother Church, it

is to be understood that divine judgment is reserved: on this no man can pronounce a clear opinion; to whom, if God has given indulgence, our severity does no harm; if he has prepared the execution, our kindness avails nothing.

8. The Apostle forbids us to be wiser than we ought to be wise (Rom. 12:3); Whoever, therefore, feels otherwise, and thinks that what he feels is right, should speak, write, and argue under this devotion of piety, especially in the business of religion, so as to compel no one to obey his words unwillingly. nor should he believe that the opinion of one man is so valid as to cause prejudice to those who feel otherwise. Each one may, by preaching the right faith, write what he feels, but not to sign what he himself had written, and challenge others. How much labored in the preaching of the word, after the apostles, those most holy and illustrious teachers, whom the Lord had granted by the Spirit of wisdom and knowledge to teach the Catholics, and to attack the heretics? yet they left their books to posterity unsigned. Let us consider what the blessed Apostle advises: Let two or three prophets speak, or examine the others (1 Cor. 14:29). Did he say: Let them sign, or be compelled to sign? He commands that what has been said be examined more carefully, lest an easy agreement fall into error: let each one be free, after having read what one man has dictated, not to accept his sayings as if they were canonical writings: but to think what he chooses, what he rejects, what he immediately follows, what he thinks with his more prudent brethren to confer; Let there be no need to create a prejudice for himself by signing, lest he afterwards feel otherwise, if afterwards the revealed truth shows us to feel otherwise: but let the pious writer patiently bear the concern of those who seek the pious truth, and not hasten to hold the hand of the hearers, but be prepared by a sweet sense to agree with those who feel better.

9. The blessed Pontiff Augustine, in the charity of Christ, gave an example of whose humility to almost all the teachers of the Catholic Church: "He will not hesitate, he says, to seek me wherever I am stuck; nor will he be ashamed to say if I am wrong. Accordingly, whoever reads these things, where he is equally sure, let him continue with me; where he hesitates at the same time, let him seek with me; when he recognizes his error, let him return to me; where mine is, he will call me back. Let us thus enter together on the path of charity, tending to him of whom it is said: Seek his face always. And this plea, pious and just before

the Lord our God. Meanwhile, with all who read what I write, etc. (*Aug. lib. 1 de Trinit. ch. 2, 3*)." For, as we have often said above, there are only divine precepts in canonical books, and paternal decrees in general synods, not to be refuted or rejected, but to be kept and embraced; the Holy Scripture instructing: Hear, my son, the law of your father, and do not reject the counsel of your mother (Prov. 1:8; 6:20). For the law of the father shines, as it seems to me, in the canonical books; the counsel of the mother is contained in the universal councils; wherefore those who meet such priests sign their statutes, so that no doubt may be left by whom the discussion was held: besides those who decide what is to be decided, no one compels them to sign any more; for it is judged to be sufficient for full confirmation, if, brought to the notice of the whole Church, they cause no offense or scandal to the brethren, but are firm in their adherence to the apostolic faith, strengthened by the consent of the apostolic see.

10. Therefore, your happiness is worthy of these three rules in the order and language in which we were able to carefully attend to the intimates, and (if it pleases our humble conviction) to keep them. That there should be no revision of the council of Chalcedon or the like; but those which have once been established shall be kept inviolable. That no scandals should arise between the living for the sake of the dead brothers. So that no one wishes to give his book, by the signatures of many, the authority which the Catholic Church has brought to the canonical books alone. This too will be able to advance the tranquility of the Churches, if no one wishes to prescribe what the Church should follow, but to hold to what the Church teaches; she said to the Lord through Moses in the song of Deuteronomy: Ask your father, and he will tell you; your elders, and they will tell you everything (Deut. 32:7). For then will also be fulfilled the sweet doctrine of the Teacher of the Gentiles, admonishing the Corinthians and saying: When you have come together, each of you has a psalm, a doctrine, an interpretation: let all things be for edification (1 Cor. 14:16). Behold, when I was questioned, I could not keep silent because of obedience, answering as a pupil to the teachers, unlearned to the learned, younger to the elders. Examine, we ask, for the sake of charity, whether this little answer could comprehend the truth; and, if indeed it pleases, let your discretion determine whether it should be disclosed to the brethren.

EPISTLE VII. TO THE KING PARAENETICUS. What a religious leader ought to be in military actions, or on the seven rules of innocence.

1. To be exercised by the labors of social life, the ignorance of childhood, as soon as a rational man becomes destitute, or begins with God, the leader of an illustrious queen, or the military age. Because of this, the Apostle Paul: No one, he says, who serves God entangles himself with worldly affairs (2 Tim. 2:4); showing that they are the soldiers of God, as they are also the soldiers of the world. The two kinds of soldiery, therefore, signify two classes of soldiers: others are bound by bodily soldiery to labor with the world, according to the will of the earthly king; others are brought by spiritual warfare to the heavenly camp through the gratuitous grace of the heavenly emperor. The soldiers of the age are subject to various passions and desires; God's soldiers crucify their flesh with vices and lusts. They are nourished by protein; these virtues They are trying to kidnap someone else; these also either patiently destroy their own, or strive mercifully to provide. They consult their own interests; these are common. They wear it whence they are exalted by false praises; these seek whence they may be honored with eternal rewards. Vanity gives them the image of joy; Truth brings true joys to these people. They hasten to save and always hold the perishing country, which is also perishing; they desire to possess that which will never perish, lest they perish for ever. To them to live is toil, and to die is punishment; to these Christ is to live, and to die is gain. They fight against visible enemies; these against the invisible. Those cruel greed; mercy makes them kind. Envy those contentious; these meekness and peace. They, through pride, fight for their own people; these, through humility, consider each other superior to themselves. Babylonia is governed by them; by these and in these the heavenly Jerusalem is administered by the Lord. And it usually happens that the soldiers of God and the soldiers of the world, united in body (though separated in mind) at the same time, feel that prosperity and adversity are temporary. But prosperity lifts up the soldiers of the world, adversity casts them down; but the soldiers of God, whether in prosperity or in adversity, persevere unmoved; because their glory is the testimony of their conscience; where they rest when the world suffers tribulations; where they are not afraid of perpetuating the enemy of continence, when there is an abundance of pleasures, the thorns of lust sprouting from the root of temporal happiness. The soldiers of God gladly hear blessed John shouting with a louder trumpet to

his fellow soldiers: Love not the world, nor the things that are in the world. If anyone loves the world, the Father's love is not in him; for all that is in the world is the lust of the flesh, and the lust of the eyes, and the ambition of the world, which is not of the Father, but is of the world. And the world passeth away, and the lust thereof: but he that doeth the will of God abideth for ever (1 John 2:15-17). To those who hear and obey this most salutary admonition, whenever the hidden dispensation of the pious Creator bestows the power to judge and dispose of the earthly republic, then in part the army of the world is not filled with graver sins: then the restless are easily rebuked, the small-minded are comforted, the weak are supported; the license of crimes is given to the unrighteous, and the innocence of doing good is allotted freedom.

2. Let us, therefore, ask with constant prayers him who arranges the world of the earth in equity, making all things according to the counsel of his will; since the Psalmist truly sings of himself: Whatever he willed, he did in heaven and on earth, in the sea and in all deep places (Ps. 134:6); that he may deign to advance his soldiers, concealed under the garb of secular military service, to the greatest dignities: ruling them within, and imparting the knowledge of ruling others; as he is known to have already given to you, the illustrious leader of the Queen. And therefore, with praiseworthy concern, you asked the venerable Fulgentius, the pontiff of the Church of Ruspens, what kind of rule should be kept for your spiritual purpose when you are busy with military actions. Wisely, surely, you would have sought the answer of wisdom from a wise man, and neither the questioner nor the question lacked holy prudence. And you already carried what he was able to teach; and he was able to teach you what you were doing, so that you would recognize your manners in his words, and he would approve of his words from your manners. But only because the dictation of the half-full book is incomplete, nothing is known to have answered this question of yours (for the beginnings of your glorious work, longer air the first question of your letters: Whether the flesh of Christ was corruptible or incorruptible; whence still disputing that excellent teacher, before he had faithfully rendered by reason of faith about military acts when he began to speak with piety, he passed to the immortal joys of eternal bliss, the Word of God, which he always had in his heart and mouth to contemplate face to face. Am I as filled with wisdom as he? Do I have the same ability to speak? Is it similar to being given a position of authority? or at least the very innocence of conversation is such for me, that I

am burdened with infirmity of mind as well as of body, entangled with past and present excesses? So what should I do? I want to satisfy your desire, but I am not able: especially when thinking and reconsidering the merits of my iniquities, I judge the neighbor of pride to lead others through the paths of justice through which I myself do not walk.

3. Woe to me, until the Most High has mercy. Behold, I, bound by the bonds of ecclesiastical service, am distracted by worldly cares; and how dare I show the law in the world of spiritual warfare? Shall I weep, or shall I speak? The life of another seems to be learned, or is it better to correct my own? The first virtue is to live well; the second is to teach rightly: but he who does not live well teaches rightly in vain; I, then, not yet living well, how can I teach rightly? Nevertheless, since man does not teach man, but God is the teacher of all, and you seek to hear not human commands, but divine ones, passing by what I am, know what you ought to be; nay, rather, be glad that you are what you are to us. 1. Believe the helper of the grace of God necessary for you through each act, saying with the Apostle: I am what I am by the grace of God (1 Cor. 15:10). 2. Let your life be a mirror, where your soldiers can see what they should do. 3. Do not desire to dominate, but to benefit. 4. Love your country as yourself. 5. Prefer the human to the divine. 6. Don't be too righteous. 7. Remember that you are a Christian.

For it seems to me that by these seven rules in military actions men can be spiritual and please God; and to suffer no loss of good conduct, but rather to advance to the greater increase of justice. If you want to be a perfect soldier of God among the soldiers of the world, hold firmly to what we have briefly said. For if you confess grace, the Spirit of the fear of the Lord will rest upon you. If your life is a mirror where the soldiers can see what they should do, the Spirit of mercy will rest on you. If you do not desire to rule, but to benefit, the Spirit of knowledge will rest upon you. For he knows that he is in charge, who wants to benefit. If you love your country as yourself, the spirit of courage will rest upon you. If you prefer the divine to the human, the Spirit of counsel will rest upon you. If you listen willingly: Do not be too righteous, the understanding of the Spirit will rest upon you. If you remember that you are a Christian, the Spirit of wisdom will rest upon you; and through the seven-fold abundance of the Spirit, the merciful God (as his faithful friend Job most truly said): In six tribulations he will deliver you; in the seventh no evil will touch you. In famine he will deliver you from death, and in war from the hand of the sword. You will be hidden from the scourge of the tongue, and you will not fear disaster when it comes. You will laugh at desolation and famine, and you will not be afraid of the beasts of the earth, but you will make a covenant with the stones of the regions, and the beasts of the earth will be peaceful to you. And you will know that your tabernacle has peace; and visiting your appearance, you will not sin (Job. 5, 19-24). It is clearly necessary that, keeping the order of the partition, you should pay attention to the one discussing these seven kinds in detail; Knowing this principally, no one understands rightly without the grace of God, no one lives justly. For the Lord gives understanding, the Lord makes whom He wills religious. We have nothing good of us: Every best thing given, and every perfect gift (contesting the apostle James) came down from the Father of lights, with whom there is no change or shadowing of importance (James 1:17).

FIRST RULE- Give all the glory to God.

4. The first rule, therefore, which you ought to keep among military acts, is that you do not ascribe anything more proud to your strength, but that all that you do wisely, or bravely, or successfully, you refer to the praise of the mighty Creator. desiring all to have virtue in holy humility. For he says: Do not say in your heart: My power and my power has done me this great power; but you will remember the Lord your God, because he gives you the power to do bravery (Deut. 8:17-18). As the prophet Jeremiah warns even more fully: Let not the wise man glory in his wisdom, and let not the mighty man glory in his strength, and let not the rich man glory in his riches; but let him glory in this: to understand and to know that I am the Lord, who do mercy, and judgment, and justice upon the earth (Jer. 9:23-24). Therefore, frequently, and (if possible) without ceasing, you will cry out with the voice of your heart and body: Lord, my strength and my helper in the day of evil (Jer. 16:19). And again: Heal me, Lord, and I will be healed; save me, and I will be saved, because you are my glory. For by saying these things, you will be seen to be following the teaching of St. Paul, who says: He who glories, let him glory in the Lord (II Cor. 10:17). And then the prophetic sentence will be fulfilled over you: Blessed is the man who trusts in the Lord, and the Lord will be his hope; and it shall be like a fruitful tree without water, and shall send forth its roots in the moisture; he will

not be afraid when the heat comes, and there will be numerous bushes in it; and in the year of drought he will not fear, and will not fail to bear fruit (Jer. 17:7-8). But he will fail if he forgets him, about whom the faithful Isaiah tells the faithful: the everlasting God, the Lord who created the borders of the earth; He will not fail, nor will he labor, nor is there a search for his wisdom. He gives strength to the weary, and increases courage and strength to those who are not. Children will fail, and they will labor, and young people will fall with infirmity. But those who hope in the Lord will change their strength, take wings like eagles; they will run and not toil, they will fly and not fail (Is. 40:28-31). Run, soldier of God, with haste, that, joined with such a number, you may carry on military affairs safely. For if it is necessary to use advice, Wisdom immediately answers you: My advice is mine, and my protection (Prov. 8:14). If you are to fight in a battle, you will hear the voice of the mighty David: The Lord saves not with the sword, nor with the spear: the war is his (I Ki. 17:47). If you arrange your guards against hostile attacks, the psalm answers the thinker: Unless the Lord guards the city, he who guards it watches in vain (Ps. 126:1). If a small army is to be led out against the innumerable multitudes of the enemy, you will immediately be strengthened by praying to Judith, and cry out in harmony with your prayer while you are groaning: Your strength is not in multitudes, nor your strength in mighty men; but thou art the God of the lowly (Judith. 9:16), the helper of the needy, the supporter of the weak. If the concord of the soldiers is sought, it will be remembered that it is written: Peace is the Lord's (Jud. 6:24). If obedience, you will sing with the voice of a psalm to the Lord your God: You will deliver me from the contradictions of the people (Ps. 17:44); but under the name of the people is also not absurdly understood a multitude of soldiers: chiefly because in such a people contradiction often abounds, and by natural severity furnishes matter for seditions. But the contradiction of the soldiers is dangerous; for it is close to murders and robberies: and sweet obedience, while it willingly obeys the salutary warnings of the wisest leader. Nor should it be doubted at all that in military acts the help of divine power is needed by the strongest leaders, as David cried, and as if in a sermon the human race responded to those who trust in their power: Blessed be the Lord my God, who teaches my hands for battle, and my fingers for war. My mercy, and my refuge, my host, and my deliverer, who subdue the peoples under me (Ps. 143:1-2). Since you understand this, when people are submitted to you by the Lord, you will undoubtedly hasten to do the will of the Lord, and you will not frighten the subjects by power alone; but you will give quiet advice to those who are obedient, taking care to be such as you wish to find others.

THE SECOND RULE- Let your life be a mirror of soldiers.

5. Indeed, the second rule is innocence when engaged in military actions, so that, as if in a mirror, the soldiers see in it what they ought to do. and imitation will provoke them to good rather than power. A wise leader must go where he wishes to lead his subjects; for that is why it is called a leader, because it leads; and he certainly deceives himself if he thinks that he can walk along the royal road, and leads them to the pit of an evil life by setting a bad example. Be thou then the standard-bearer of the most holy discipline; you erect a trophy of valor; you must appear to be imitated, and whoever hears you commanding, will not rebuke you for acting differently. Always place in your heart the words of the Apostle who said: You are inexcusable, O man, every one who judges; for in that in which you judge another, you condemn yourself; for you do the same things that you judge (Rom. 2:1). And whatever blameworthy things you pronounce, you will try first to avoid, then to condemn: whatever praiseworthy things, work first, then command. For the life of the best leader, when compared to a mirror, is well looked at, if it shines in it, not with a pretended color, but with a very true display, faith, justice, mercy, patience, self-control, and not an imprudent estimation of the future. You will be a faithful leader if you are tested by the judgment of the wise, not by the words of flatterers, and you are known to believe correctly, to deceive no one, to fulfill your promises. But you will be a just leader, if you are tried by the judgment of the wise, and not by the words of flatterers, and you are known to punish those who persist in wickedness, to favor the good, to distinguish the merits of each, and to repay the dues of all. You will be a merciful leader, if by the judgment of the wise, not by the words of flatterers, you are proved and known to love the poor, to govern your subjects, to minister to the needy, to pardon those who ask pardon, to teach wisdom to the foolish, to call back those who walk in wickedness from their evil ways, to pray to God for your enemies, to pacify those who are at odds. You will be a patient leader if, by the judgment of the wise, not by the praise of flatterers, you prove yourself and know that you work for the interests of others without the profit of greed, suffer and do no wrongs, have no lust for revenge, are in no way broken by the fear of adversity, are in no

way carried away by the desire of prosperity, persevere in those things which you have well assumed; to hope for the mercy of God, even if he delayed his coming; to do nothing quickly without planning; to receive obediently whatever the superior commands; whatever you order the inferior to arrange without disturbance. You will be a restrained leader if, by the judgment of the wise, not by the praises of flatterers, you are tested and made to know that you neither covet nor take away the things of others while you are able; to do nothing violently, nothing fraudulently, nothing without manner, nothing for pleasure, nothing for avarice, nothing forbidden by the laws or custom contrary to the state or nation, if the custom itself is neither harmful to religion nor contrary to good morals. Otherwise, an evil habit, like an ancient disease, kills unless it is driven out. The virtue of continence is to do nothing against custom, but what is good. But indeed, if you are a sovereign leader, you will also be found to be a not imprudent thinker of the future, either by watching against the plots of the adversaries, or by knowing which events are usually assigned to individual matters, whence seditions arise, whence new wars are born, whence the dissolution of severity, whence the harmful license of robberies, such as these let all things cut off at their roots open the way of the wisest leader of the quietest disposition.

6. We must also listen to the faithful advice of John the Baptist, which the soldiers heard when they asked them: What shall we also do? He did not say: Go, lay down your arms, flee from the fighting of wars, spend your time alone in prayer, despise the emperor's precepts, but he proposed other things to be observed, saying: Shake no one, do not slander anyone, be content with your wages (Luke 3:14). But to shake is to openly do violence, to slander, to seek an opportunity to do harm. For he who will not be satisfied with his wages, either breaks the reins of discipline at the same time, or robs others by rash excesses (and St. John, forbidding this, said: You shall not shock anyone), or requires causes of offense in order to frighten the innocent under some color of justice, and of his avarice, or rather of rapacity compels to satisfy the unwilling; forbidding which Saint John said: You have slandered no one. And having removed the perversity of this double malice, he added what should have followed: Be content with your wages. Blessed will be the soldiers if they keep these precepts; happy is the republic, if it deserves to have such soldiers; blessed is the leader in whose army many such things happen to be: nevertheless, he will

appear more blessed if he himself is such, that is, shaking no one, doing no slander to anyone, content with his wages. For surely the greater his dignity, the more he can shake and slander, and not be content with his wages. From this, however, in general, affliction arises in most states, from this the gravest cruelties, from this the savings elaborated by a thousand arts of profit, from this the venality in the judgments, from this the laxity in the battles, from this the diminution of the whole republic, if the leader begins not to be content with his wages, and on top of the public benefits, private ones are enlarged desiring advantages, he cares only for his own benefit, but neglects the safety or security of his subjects. Such a leader is not around his equals, both modest and sweet, but quarrelsome and avaricious; He is not gentle, common and easy around the inferiors, but cruel, accepting of persons and difficult. Under this the discipline of the soldiers quickly deteriorates; For whom do they wish to spare the soldiers of the provincials, whom they have seen to suffer fraud from the leader himself? How will they be satisfied with their wages, who feel that their leader is ennobled by foreign resources? When a leader strikes someone, doesn't he use the same officers for violence? When he slanders someone, does he practice fraud through them? Therefore, by commanding them often iniquity, he causes equity to despise them. Does a wise leader want to be a quiet, peaceful and submissive soldier? let him himself be just, merciful, temperate, and in his administration love not to preside, but to benefit. Let him imitate Samuel in good deeds; He compares to himself the free confidence of a shy and honorable liberty, so that he may be able to say with a frank face to his subjects, as Samuel said: Behold, I am here; answer against me in the presence of the Lord, and in the presence of his Christ; if I have taken someone's calf, or taken someone's ass, or I have harmed any of you by power, or I have oppressed someone, or I have taken from someone's hand for a prayer or a shoe. Answer me, and I will repay you (1 Ki. 12, 2, 3). And let him also answer what they said to Samuel: You did not harm any of us, nor did you oppress anyone by power, nor did you break us, nor did you take anything from our hands. Oh, how glorious a leader will be before the face of a prince who deserves to hear these things! The nobles will magnify him, the humble will bless him, fame will follow him better than all riches. He will be given, as it is written, the chosen gift of faith, and a more peaceful lot in the temple of God, the fruits of good labor and a good reputation (Wis. 3:14). And if perhaps he is removed, or ordered not to administer the republic, he will remain and continue in the love of all as if he were present. But whoever succeeds him will find nothing to criticize, but something to marvel at. However, he loves to benefit more than to rule. For many rules, but very few benefit the people over whom they rule. Anyone who is encumbered with private honors, scorning the interests of his subjects, desires to preside rather than to benefit. But such a leader is useless and unjust: he can neither govern a standing republic, nor repair a collapsed one.

THE THIRD RULE You do not desire to dominate, but to benefit.

7. The third rule, therefore, is innocence when engaged in military actions, if you are therefore presiding over it, as you say. But you will be seen to benefit if you understand the time and place of your administration. And you will indeed consider the time, while you judge with wise discretion whether it will be peaceful or disturbed by the tumults of war. For often what the warrior pursues by discipline in the leisure of peace, patience patiently endures amid crowds and swords. But you will rightly consider the place, whether it is barren or fertile; whether he is sufficient for the nourishment of an army, or less suitable; whether it should appear desolate and uncultivated, or unshaken and carefully prepared. For whenever a place where you seem to command an army needs repair, all private gains are to be despised, even those which custom already freely claims for itself; and to moderate the criticism of severity a little more rigidly. In addition to this, you will be seen to benefit in two ways, if you do no harm to anyone, and prevent those who are in the habit or want to do harm as much as you can, nay, as much as Christ has given you to be able. And then the best leader will not harm anyone, if in all his headquarters some friend, client, physician, squire, or someone always attached to the side of the leader because of devotion to public office, does not dare to sell the benefits granted. For what does it help the poor, if a leader exhibits the restraint of a good leader, and another makes an opportunity for himself out of his power to satisfy his greed? Let him have such associates or servants as he knows he ought to be. For whoever is familiarly attached to a leader, to whom he entrusts many tasks, is the leader's hand; and by merit whatever they receive is believed to pass to him without doubt: nor can the reputation of a good leader be good when there have been bad ministries. Then, how will he correct strangers, unless he first corrects his own? Who doubts that those appointed in the army will jump more easily to commit crimes, if they see that the assistants of the commander are more permitted to perpetrate worse things? but all the common people will

easily guard, however indomitable the army, because the men have kept very familiar to the leader. Let him therefore take care and be careful that no one harms the wretched of his people; and while he thinks himself good, he will be thought evil for the sake of evil; to whom it is either to be said to favor, or to agree with, when they have done such things in his presence, such as, even if he himself did not do, he would not be believed to have, but to feign goodness. A wise leader cannot be excused from ignorance, whenever he may perhaps say: I do not know, I have not heard, no one's complaint has reached me. For through him we must inquire what is being done by his own people; because no one dares accuse them of public disturbances, the violence of which some fear, others tolerate. There is no doubt, then, that the most active inquisitor becomes a leader, to whom authority is born from this diligence of public severity; so that it is entirely beneficial, when he allows no one to be harmed either by himself or by another. It is possible, clearly, through this care, to acquire a good reputation, so that even if a superior person wishes to injure his subjects, he may come to the aid of free intercession; and let him easily persuade those whom he himself first spared to be spared.

8. Now the way of discussion led us to this point, where we would say that it is necessary for good leaders, even by suggesting to the princes that it is beneficial to the subjects. For we know that most people, in order to please those who are superior, consult less with those who are inferior. I think that they are of the number of those who govern the provinces, concealing their wants or tribulations, and announce that whatever they see falling is safe to continue, thinking that their glory if they lie to stand what they know has perished. But they are compelled to show their credulity by impious words, and to multiply the losses of the poor provincials; by which they appear to be gains, but are absolutely hostile to the republic, to provide for the most pious princes, rather hindering the restoration of the country. And where they manage to appear useful, there they are completely useless. For by imposing heavier burdens, they make tired peoples succumb; nor do they leave to their successors anything but mourning and tears. I don't want you to be found like them. If you love to benefit, not to dominate, do something worthy of memory, that posterity will remember, and that your times will not be forgotten. Take care to leave the rich whom you find poor, to provide abundance where you too have suffered scarcity; and if indeed your strength is sufficient, restore the province without

delay; but if the will is present for the most pious work, but the ability is lacking, bring this to the consciousness of a superior power. Be a faithful witness to the miseries of others. Supplicate, beseech, until you obtain help. By asking for long labors, others may not endure long hardships by toil; for you will be judged to have provided whatever the university demands of you. Do not appear to be willing to please the hour; those who see, or feel, or sometimes even endure in the provinces where evils are at war, report good things through false reports, thinking that they will receive the most joyful news, so that they may appear either useful to the administration they carry on, or necessary. O wretched iniquity! While they seek to preside, they do not think of profiting; but those who are deprived of honor try to preserve their unjust power through the inconvenience of others. But they are sometimes deceived by the cunning of malicious ambition, when public fame begins to speak of what they are silent about, and they are found to have been liars in their profession. May God always prevent this insanity and these behaviors from the best leaders who love to benefit, not to be in charge!

FOURTH RULE- Love your country as yourself.

9. For then the republic is well governed, and can be saved from great dangers, if its leader loves it as much as he loves himself. Indeed, it is a clear sentence of the old law: Love your neighbor as yourself (Lev. 19:18): which Paul, a suitable preacher of the New Testament, confirms and renews by repeating thus: All the law is fulfilled in one word; in that you love your neighbor as yourself (Gal. 5:14). And who is to be esteemed a better neighbor to the wisest leader than the republic, to whom both business, state, and health are entrusted? Let him therefore love her as himself, because by loving her as himself, he will long to see her peaceful, quiet, fruitful, tranquil without any disturbance, just as he certainly strives as much as he can to be peaceful, quiet, rich, and calm without any disturbance. Therefore, you, best of men, whenever you think of what you ought to be in military actions, enter into the broadest recesses of your conscience. See there how you wish to have joy; and take care carefully, that the republic, which you love as yourself, may not suffer any sadness. Consider that you do not want any harm to happen to you, nor pain, nor disgrace: and hasten to rescue the republic from these evils. If it displeases you when you yourself suffer violence in private, you ought to hate those whose violence afflicts the

commonwealth. If you are afraid to endure the robbery of your goods, take away the habit of robbery from the robbers. If you detest, and truly think you are an enemy, whoever has sought you with false accusations, judge the detestable accusers of the whole province. Or perhaps it is difficult to judge, so that the whole province is tolerated by the accusers? Believe me, it often happens. His accusers are ambitions, to whom, in order to be given power to oppress the poor, they promise impossible things; and to the desolated regions, also destroyed by the onslaught of war, they ascribe a state of former stability; all lying still flourishing, still being able to support not only the usual functions, but also new ones, if added, the burdens of taxes. Now they blame the ministers of the fiscal exaction in secret whispers, and neglecting them, or letting them go too far, they willfully lie to provide no gains for the republic; But (O obstinate desire!) their diligence, their cruelty; reason, it is better called predation. That is why they want to buy the most serious actions, because they are thinking of selling; they promise falsehoods in order to steal the truths; they are flattered to do harm; they exercise a pious concern for the public interests, but at the same time they intend to afflict and deteriorate everything. They desire to overthrow, not to govern; to dissipate, not to preserve; to devour, not to feed. They furnish matter for seditions, increases for miseries, cause for weeping: doing this, when the province is almost dead, that it may not die more slowly. Cover your ears with thorns (Eccl. 28:28); do not listen to the voice of those who speak evil. When you see them praise the fertility of the fields, tell of the abundance of rains, and frequently describe pleasant places, fear a flattering story. The word of this kind of entry is: the will of a good leader must by no means stick to it. And do not think that it is necessary whether they tell something truthfully; for the artificer is no less careful to do harm by the habit of vices, although they know that everything has perished, yet they seek some places quite rare, which, with the mercy of the Lord protecting them, deserved to be preserved either unharmed, or perhaps a little damaged. Reciting the names of those commended to memory most frequently, they diminish by comparison the greatness of the general calamity, and say (as you could prove without doubt): The province is sufficient for these functions; for that place has only utility. O wretched ones whose mouth has spoken vanity, and their right hand, the right hand of iniquity (Ps. 143:8)! If their eyes are open to their good, why do the people groan? Let them see if the balance is just on their lips. First let them count how many have perished, and afterwards how many remain. Do they see nothing there where piety is needed; and they mark this with anxious lights, whence is envy generated?

10. Make your way far from them, they may always find your house closed. Let them dislike you by suggesting harm, and let them know that they dislike you. Indeed, even the worst group of detractors adheres to them in a familiar way, who secretly whisper to the best leaders foreign abilities; so that, captivated by the snares of avarice, they may lose faith in pious administration, if they acquiesce in impious persuasions, and think of taking away what they are told. What else but slander is raised against innocent men? Indeed, the human race is detestable and extremely abominable, traitors. In whose headquarters they did not emerge at all, he loves the republic as himself; unwilling to do to others what he himself would not suffer. For this is the fourth rule of innocence when engaged in military actions, which you hold and ought to hold firmly, that you may love the republic as yourself, free charity. Moses, filled with the abundance of sweetness, while he saw that the people of Israel, that is, his own republic, had sinned against Almighty God, and he feared the future severity of the most just judges, thus took the angry one to appease him: I beseech you, O Lord, if you forgive their sin, forgive but if not, remove me from your book which your hands have written (Ex. 32:31). Let us consider what it would have profited Moses to save others, if he perished. But because he always loved the republic as himself, he appeased God by this sacrifice of charity; and neither himself perished, nor did he allow the people whom he ruled to perish. Saint David imitated this with equal power of love, striking the city with an angel: Let thy hand be turned upon me, and upon my father's house. What did those who are sheep do (II Ki. 42:17)? Give a man who loves the republic in this way, and you will see how much he pleases God, even when he is occupied with military actions. Indeed, you are worthy to live like such, ready to labor for the rest of your subjects; ready even to suffer death, if God permits, in order to free your subjects from the danger of death. Fear more, best leader, that the province becomes worse, than yourself poorer by diminishing resources: judge good reputation by inestimable riches. Nevertheless, since every man who loves himself must love God more than himself (in other words, he who loves God less does not love, but hates himself), whoever loves the republic as himself, loves God more than the republic, and prefers divine affairs to human affairs.

LETTERS & PAMPHLETS

FIFTH RULE- Prefer the divine to the human.

11. And this will be the fifth rule of innocence when occupied with military actions, so as to consider temporal things, so as to pay more attention to the eternal; so as to consult with present acts, that he may think more of future rewards. For it frequently happens, which you cannot ignore, by the Spirit of wisdom revealing everything to your senses, that necessity compels something to be done which the eternal law forbids, for example, lest we set forth unknown examples: if several heretics are found in the strongest army, vindicating the false opinion of unbelief with stubborn animosity, and for this reason the Catholic leader should be advised to spare or consult the heretics, or to give permission to preachers of nefarious error to practice blasphemies, bearing patiently, because of the scandal which he fears to suffer, even those polluted by the wash of the second baptism, already reborn once; that is to say, by consenting to such an evil suggestion, although it may seem that he has provided some benefit of temporal goods to his subjects, he has in the meantime harmed himself; while judging that he had little hope of the help of God, he sometimes endures dangers worse than he fears; and not being steadfast in his faith, he competently exercises the zeal of religion, nor escapes the fall of the gravest tribulation, because he preferred the earthly to the heavenly, and he in no way hesitated to offend the will of the Creator, wishing to please men who were corrupt in mind. You will be happy, then, if, occupied with military actions, you flatter no one for the true faith you hold; and prevent the dogs coming from the factory of lies to bark against her: putting your hope in him whose power no one resists with impunity; which, if you offend, you presume without reason from the multitude of the army; if you have mercy, you will fear neither a proud soldier, nor a violent enemy. Your main concern, then, is to be occupied with military actions, so that the Catholic faith may always conquer its adversaries. Defend her between arms and swords, persuade her to the minds of the armed.

12. But the Catholic faith is that the Father, the Son, and the Holy Spirit preach one substance or essence against Arius, three persons against Sabellius; so that when unity in essence is well understood, and property in persons, true equality also in majesty may be adored. For there are three, because there is one Father, another Son, and another Holy Spirit. But these three are one, and they are

supremely one, because individually God is the Father, God the Son, God the Holy Spirit: yet there are not three gods, but one God, of whom the Holy Scripture says: Hear, Israel, the Lord your God is one God (Deut. 6:4). For the Trinity removes the suspicion of a solitary God, and shows to believers one God in one substance. It is not so one, that by each half full, the whole becomes in all, and therefore is one; but one in number, kind, power, and fullness. As he has in all things, so he does not lack in each. As much in the Father alone as in the Son and the Holy Spirit; as much in the Son alone as in the Father and the Holy Spirit; as much in the Holy Spirit as in the Father and the Son. As much in each of them as in two. As much in two as in three. As much in three as in each. For there is nothing arranged by degrees, nothing different in quality, nothing small in quantity, nothing separated in place, nothing later in time, nothing ineffective, nothing susceptible. Wherein this only receives the distinction that they are to each other, that is, the Father to the Son, the Son to the Father, the Holy Spirit to those of whom and with whom both the Spirit and the Holy are, that He alone in the Trinity may be called holy; and it is the property of the Father to beget, the property of the Son to be born, and the property of the Holy Spirit to proceed from both. For the Father of one Son is the Father, the Son of the one Father is the Son, and the Holy Spirit is the Spirit of both the Father and the Son. The generation belongs to the Father alone, the birth to the Son alone, and the Holy Spirit alone to each of these processions. It is worth while the necessity of our salvation waited, that for the sake of liberating men God the man should be born of man, the Father was not born according to the flesh, because the Son never was, nor the Holy Spirit, who was neither the Father at any time nor the Son. But the Son was born so that he himself might become the son of a Virgin mother, who is the Son of God the Father: and through the temporal birth of God Almighty, the number of children would in no way increase, nor would the second birth of the only Son make two sons. Above all, because he is the same one Son, coeternal, consubstantial, and equal with the eternal Father, who alone had to become the son of man, after the fullness of the time had come, that man should be made of woman, redeeming men and women, born temporally of one sex to save both, by choosing one in whom he was born, another whence he was born, so he received the truth of our substance, so as not to duplicate the singularity of his person, the giants of two substances, but still of one and the same person. For the Word was before the flesh, one nature, and one person; The Word made flesh, of two natures, and one person. The Word before the flesh, homousion to the Father; The word made flesh was homousion both to the Father and to the mother. The Word was ineffably begotten before the flesh without the beginning of time; The Word became flesh after the fullness of time had come, wonderfully and singularly, without the disease of lust. The Word before the flesh making a new world; The Word made flesh, redeeming the world. The Word before the flesh, making divine; The Word made flesh, at the same time making divine, and suffering human, as he willed. The Word before the flesh, the only begotten God; The word made flesh, Emmanuel, which is translated God with us. Yet the same Himself, the Word made flesh, who in the beginning was the Word, and the Word was with God, and God was the Word: for man was not God, but God became man that man might be God, that is Christ Jesus. When he was in the form of God, he did not presumptuously think that he was equal to God, but emptied himself, taking the form of a servant, being made in the likeness of men, and found in the habit of a man. He humbled himself by becoming obedient to the point of death, the death of the cross. Because of this God exalted him and gave him a name which is above every name. that in the name of Jesus every knee should bow, of the heavenly, the earthly, and the infernal; and let every tongue confess that the Lord Jesus Christ is in the glory of God the Father (Phil. 2:6-11).

13. This is the Lord Jesus, who in the perfect Trinity is called the Son, when we are commanded to be baptized in the name of the Father and of the Son and of the Holy Spirit. This is great and small, high and low, impassive and susceptible, immortal and mortal, living without sin among men and passing away the sins of men: in all things like us without sin, and in all things like the Father, who sent him to us in the likeness of sinful flesh. and of sin he condemned sin in the flesh. Truly and properly the Son of God the Father, truly and properly the Son of the Virgin Mother. Above the heavens is the life of the living, above the earth the medicine of the sick, among the underworld the resurrection of the dead. Mediator of God and men, because of two substances, or natures, of which he is one with God, and the other common with us. In one and the same person, in whom he became the true mediator, not having the beginning of divinity from Mary; but having from it the material of the flesh which he received in order to be born. Having the flesh of our kind, not airy, not fanciful, not deposited from heaven, not made from elsewhere: although human, polluted in no part by the filth of original iniquity,

not from the pleasure of flesh and blood, but formed by the coming power of the Holy Spirit, and quickened by the inspiration of the rational soul. Properly and truly human, that is, of the mother, but still without a human father. Corruptible, because he felt hunger, thirst, pain, and death voluntarily, but nevertheless truly. Incorruptible, because he felt no offense in himself, either original or personal, and consented to iniquity with no desire to be defeated. Nor could the burial come to the corruption of putrefaction, by the grace of the resurrection: when, bearing the fetters of the underworld, the same Christ himself always arose, for forty days he conversed with the disciples, and thus miraculously ascended to heaven. Where he is just sitting at the right hand of the Father, he will come in glory, who had previously come in humility: he will judge the living and the dead, and condemn the unbelieving; but to those who believe he will bestow remission of sins, and eternal life, if they continue in the Catholic Church, cleansed from the contagion of all vices. Indeed, the Catholic Church is the station where the good doctor heals our wounds. He is the son of the promise, whosoever claims it unto the shedding of blood.

14. Therefore, an excellent and faithful leader, keep all his dogmas, preach, avenge, lead to it those willing, compel those unwilling, not with the pain of executions, not with fear of the fierce sword, but with modest rebuke and severity full of love. Far away is the fear of the devil. Let the heretics know that you are a Catholic; let the Catholics know that you detest heretics. In the days of your administration, let the assembly of sinners fail, let the number of the elect increase. If he is made glorious by whose labor the boundaries of the empire are extended, how much more glorious will he be whose labor the Catholic Church is multiplied? Rejoice in the gains of Christ, grieve in the expenses. And let the sentence of the apostle Peter always remain in your heart, blaming the leaders under this question: Whom, he says, must we obey? To God or to men (Acts 5:29)? So you, faithful leader, whenever the fervor of your faith causes the profane soldiers to stumble, say with your mouth and heart: Whom must we obey? To God or to men? But your conscience answering: To God, speak, do, ordain what God loves; so that those who already exist who are contrary to the truth, either follow willingly, or remain murmuring, and are powerless against the orthodox religion. For on the other hand they will not be able to lack those whom you please in good works, whose hearts cling more tenaciously to you. Faith has true lovers everywhere. No matter how much

iniquity is exalted, truth prevails. But let us suppose that perhaps in the multitude of the army there are many heretics, and few Catholics: you ought rather to rely on the strongest forces, so that, if the grace of God should permit, you may make all the strongest soldiers Catholics, or at least let a few heretics go. I still speak a little. Perhaps you have been sent to those regions where you will not find any Orthodox, or at least the most rare and hidden ones. There, too, manfully sow the word of life to the glory of Christ. do not think first how you will govern them by imperial laws, but how you will correct them by spiritual discourses: and, terrified by the name of authority, first prevent them from resisting the holy doctrine, and then gradually persuade them to agree. It is useful for you to feel right, if you do not leave others also in wrongdoing. The instance of a good leader generally afforded many an opportunity of salvation. But if perhaps you despair that they can be saved, it is good to preach the concordance of salvation; because God crowns the will, not the ability. Sowing belongs to the duty of the diligent farmer; It is the duty of heaven to make the earth fruitful, and to respond to the wishes of its worshiper. In this way, with regard to your subjects, you will easily use your energy even to the highest powers, and to those whose office you are the leader of the kings, if by any chance they feel contrary to the true faith, and you will not be able to give in, and resist, you will learn to be ready for martyrdom. Otherwise, anyone who, fearing to offend the inferiors, does not follow the cause of his own religion, how will he deserve to sing with the prophet David: I spoke of your testimonies in the presence of kings, and I was not confused (Ps. 118:46)?

15. Oh, if good leaders would begin to put the divine before the human, they would provide remedies for the greatest errors. This virtue is widespread, it is poured out through more and more paths of justice. Prefer the divine to the human; and the widow should not endure oppression, because of the hope of a passing gain; the guardian's substance should not be in the least need of favor; the unjust litigator loses the worst victory; He was willing to listen to the demands of the priests. The prayer will be frequent. The interest in reading, despite the busyness rushing in from all sides, boils with the fire of spiritual desire (removed from warmth). Why does a good leader oppress a widow? Why does he allow the pupil to be hurt? Why does he judge for an unjust litigant? Why does he hardly or rarely go to church? Why doesn't he read? but because he prefers the human to the divine? Therefore always prefer the divine to the

human; all your religious will and deeds and words, even though they are military acts, will be safe. But who could offer the sacrifice of alms in such a way as the best leader, to whom the greatness of his power affords abundant opportunities for bestowing mercy, if, however, he prefers the divine to the human? Did Daniel the prophet Nebuchadnezzar say in vain: May my counsel please you, O king, and redeem your sins with alms, and your injustices with the compassion of the poor; and will God spare your sins (Dan. 4:24)? but since the ease of alms is more powerful than the powerful? To whom, too, according to the kind of almsgiving, is it possible to work any longer, that is to say, to forgive those who transgress? For they more laudably pardon them, whose wrath is the harbinger of death. They love their enemies more gloriously, from whom it is lawful to demand the vengeance of blood. You have power over both works of mercy, if you prefer the divine to the human. And in this you will be most recognized to put the divine before the human, when you swear falsely to no one, and do not deceive anyone with a subtle sacrament. Although he is an ancient enemy, although he has instilled the atrocities of the republic into his bowels, he does not seem to be deceived by false oaths; even if his life hinders, let death be the cause of peace; not even if, most excellent leader, you are challenged to swear falsely. So to one man, so to the people, so to the many nations with whom you undertake to wage war, or persevering without an oath, assume the struggle; or in no way dare to liberate or help the republic by committing a crime in violation of the sacrament. For what good is it to him to conquer, whom the devil has conquered, so that he should swear falsely in the hope of victory? It is good that you should always prefer the divine to the human, and speak freely and gladly with the voice of Saint Job: As the waves of the sea hung over me, so I feared God (Job 31:23). Because of this the Psalmist sang: Lord, who will dwell in your tabernacle? or who will rest on your holy mountain (Ps. 14:1)? He answers to himself from the person of God with such words: He who speaks the truth in his heart, who has not dealt deceitfully with his tongue, nor done evil to his neighbor, nor accepted reproach against his neighbor; he who swears to his neighbor and does not deceive. He therefore shall dwell in the tabernacle of the Lord, and shall rest in his holy mountain, who swears to his neighbor and does not deceive. But he swears to his neighbor and does not deceive, whoever swears by words fulfills with deeds. But no one thinks that an enemy to whom he swears should not be deputed as a neighbor; for on this account he swears that he will be counted next. From whom, then, he wishes to be made a friend, and embraces the law of peace, he is already near; and now he who swears faithfully, swears to his neighbor, and does not deceive.

16. A false oath is the worst sin, and if you consider it a little more deeply, it is always useless, especially to those who lead an army. For the changeable hearts of young people are frequently bound by the bond of the sacrament, so that they may undertake battles with a stable faith; and then let the generals have firm security, if the fear of religion does not allow the soldiers to swear falsely. How grave, then, and how pernicious, that they may see or feel that the sacrament is easily dissolved, and that their leaders may be invited to esteem perjury as a light example? Therefore, whatever you affirm by interceding with an oath, always observe the law; whether you promise grace to the enemy, or pardon to the guilty, or rewards to those who labor with you; and this, by using the invocation of the name of God, make it credible by working; with no consideration of advantage, and fear of no danger, you must make it void. Let the word be fixed and unchangeable, the witness of whose faith God is used. There is one clear reason for breaking an oath, if you swear something in anger, so that you may offend the God by whom you are swearing. For example, if you swear that you can never be satisfied for the delinquents; if you threaten the destruction of the state, or the people, by swearing; if we should not pray deeply in the church; or other things which the divine fear forbids, the execution of the oath by the weakness of the human temptation at present overcome: then the oath is clearly not to be fulfilled, because there you do not put the human before the divine, but rather contemplate the divine; so that he may regret having sworn thus, while he is ashamed to fulfill what he has sworn. Even so, since the divine are preferred to the human, and the rule of those words will begin to be held, which forbids men to swear quickly, nay, never willing to swear: Do not, says the Gospel, swear, neither by heaven nor by earth: but let your speech be, it is, no, no (Matthew 5:34). Of course, whoever works, there is an imitator of the Son of God himself, of whom the blessed Paul speaks thus: There is not in him IS and NOT; but the IS was in him always (2 Cor. 1:18, 20). For he is immutable, like the true God, and naturally one God with the Father and the Holy Spirit. The most faithful Moses, inquiring about whose name, trembled and heard the voice of the heavens speaking to him: I am who I am. And you shall say to the children of Israel: He who has sent me to you (Ex. 3:14). Indeed, it is a great glory to abide in him who is, to follow him

who is: and because our weak nature makes us changeable, we cannot be compared to the unchangeable God by an equal power, so that as he is always in us, so we also may be able to be in him. at least let our speech be, yes is, no no; and whether by intervening in the oath, or by ceasing it, we strive to continue in the most certain truth. For the truth is divine, whence the Son of God said very truthfully: I am the truth (John 14:6). And as we remember that John said of charity: He that abideth in charity, and God abideth in him (1 John 4:16); in the same way, if we want to say, we are not lying: He who abides in the truth abides in God, and God abides in him. Let us, then, prefer the truth to all temporal interests, and then we shall rightly be found to prefer the divine to the human. Either reason clearly demonstrates the truth to us, or the divinely inspired Scripture recommends it, or the faithful teaching of the priests shows it. For under the guise of truth falsity is generally vindicated; and unless good leaders have a pious humility of heart, so that whenever they seek the truth, they remove the power of secular dignity, they will miserably put the human before the divine; that he dares recklessly, though a leader, yet a disciple of the Church, to teach the Church; nor to follow the judgments of the priests, but preferring rather to judge by the judgments of the priests.

17. We came to this place on a certain occasion, as far as I think it is necessary for the willing to always put the divine before the human. As a good leader, indeed, in all things, if you are pious and wise, you consult the Church, you make haste to obey the priests, without their counsel you do nothing without whose prayers you are helped. Above all, however, among the duties of religion, you must learn to bear only obedience: and if any scruple moves your mind, you will not easily follow your own opinion, nor will you try to persuade others, unless you first acknowledge that it has pleased the priests. Remember what God speaks to you in Deuteronomy: Ask your father, and he will tell you; your priests, and they will tell you everything (Deut. 32:7). Therefore consult those whom the Lord God of knowledge has reminded that they should be consulted. Even if you have the fullness of knowledge, if you have the ability to speak more, bow your neck to the purpose of holy humility, consult the priests. And counsel by piously asking, not violently commanding what they should answer. And let it never please you to rescind the decrees of the canons in the provinces where you exercise leadership. For if you are afraid to transgress the public laws which man has established, how will you try to meet the definitions

of the Holy Spirit? Do you not know that the Fathers, moved by the Holy Spirit, spoke; and perhaps the apostolic rebuke can be competently adapted to us: They have a zeal for God, but not according to knowledge (Rom. 10:2). Therefore, wishing to have the zeal of God according to knowledge, keep the right order, beware of the perverse. The right order is that the priests should teach, and the laity should be taught; and everyone who boasts that he belongs to the Church lives by the laws of the Church, especially those which antiquity strengthened; Hence even a custom without law, which the tradition of the holy Church has handed down to posterity from time to time to be kept, seems to be kept with the same reverence, and in no way to be removed if it is not contrary to the true faith. And let not your minds be offended by the different customs of the churches, while the faith is one. For in small minds and almost fools, this vice creeps in, the custom of their Church, where either they were born or nurtured, to seek in other Churches; and if he sees any discrepancy in custom, he suddenly suffers a breach of faith. But you, wise man, of the Church to which you have come, if you approve of the faith, immediately follow the custom, and do not usurp any newness of the sacred rite. For if a changed custom offends thee, it may likewise offend the people, whose will the best leader always hastens to conciliate in good things: frequently recalling the apostolic words, where it is written: Be ye without offense, to the Jews and to the Greeks, and to the Church of God (1 Cor. 10, 32). It seems better, therefore, lest any stumbling-block should be given to the gospel of Christ, when the multitude of the Christian people are offended, patiently, as a wise leader, endure your offense, until you either take account of another custom (in which you are offended) in any way, or receive love, if, however, as is often said, no the danger of faith is feared. For that which is not contrary to faith, this alone must be borne with equanimity, that is, for the offense of the people: because this also certainly belongs to the guarding of the faith, to avoid the offense of the people. For a people offended easily leaps to schisms, and you know how all faith is endangered in schisms. It is therefore good that, favoring you, agreeing with you, and in no way forbidding you, according to the most pious definitions of the Fathers, each Church should follow its custom: and you should become a partaker of that custom held by the Church where you have been converted for the time or the necessity of administration. Otherwise, being accustomed to love, and extremely unusual to fear, justice is too much, worthy not of praise, but of censure, if it pleases the sentence of the wisest Solomon: Be not righteous much; nor be wise more than is necessary, lest you be astonished (Ecc. 7:17). What is it, lest you be astonished? Don't stay cold. Who stays cool? From whom the fervor of charity is withdrawn. So don't be too righteous.

SIXTH RULE- Don't be just a lot.

18. And this should be the sixth rule of innocence for you, when you are occupied with military actions. For whatever you say, do, or arrange, so as to please God and men, and with the fervency of charity wonderfully shut out the cold of iniquity, do not be much just, nor wise more than is necessary. Does anyone who is guilty of the most serious crime deserve to feel judicial censure? Temper, leader very well, the onslaught of severity; and while punishments are being inflicted on the accused, let pity say in his inner ears: Do not be too righteous (Ibid.). Another forgetful friendship, failed to show due duties? He deserves to be cast away, he deserves to feel a rough wound; drink, I beseech you, the right pain, do not reciprocate the like. Do not esteem as an enemy, but rebuke still as a friend; Answering the most wise Solomon to you: Do not be too righteous. So be just, but don't be too just. Be just, that you may rebuke the restless; do not be too just, that you may comfort the small-minded, that you may receive the weak, and be patient with all. Consider with whom you command, and how hard hearts you desire to bend; so that by only threatening, only by striking, only by granting pardons, you may by no means let the sins of the soldiers remain unpunished, and yet you may not always requite their excesses with fitting punishments, saying to yourself: Do not be too just. How much, most wise leader, are to be dissembled, how much to be tolerated, how much to be lightly touched, how much to be granted by the intercession of the priests, from him who wisely hears: Do not be too righteous! You may consider in silence different kinds of vices, for the cure of which he wished to foresee a remedy, who said: Be not much righteous. Indeed, among other things, we shall not wound anyone with the hidden arrow of detraction, nor shall we more anxiously inquire into the character of those who live well where they are to blame, if the faithful Scripture speaks to each one of us through the Holy Spirit: Be not much righteous. Because, of course, he guiltily strives to be just in a great deal, who examines the life of his neighbor through all justice, putting aside the consideration of human frailty; as if he were able to live without sin, whoever begins to avoid sins; especially confirming James the apostle: For in

many things we all stumble (James 3:2); Hence the proud detractor is not undeservedly recalled from the exaltation of judging, when it is said to him: Do not be too righteous; that he may gladly fulfill what Paul, the vessel of choice and the teacher of the nations, says: If a man is preoccupied with some offense, you who are spiritual, instruct him in the spirit of meekness; considering yourself, lest you also be tempted (Gal. 6:1). This is therefore: Do not be too righteous, which is: Consider yourself, lest you also be tempted. Moreover, he who is thus enraged at transgressors, as if he himself were considered completely ignorant of transgressions, immediately falls miserably into the pit of cruelty. And crying out to the aforementioned apostle: Bear one another's burdens, and thus you will fulfill the law of Christ; By patiently bearing the burden of no one, he becomes importunate to all, and gradually increasing the hatred of many, he opens the door first to seditions, then to public battles; desiring to be much just, he really became unjust, and unworthy of the name or office of a leader. The necessary discourse, therefore, most excellent leader, I often repeat, and this sixth rule of innocence, occupied with military actions, I forcefully emphasize to you: Do not be too righteous. Piety is useful for all things (1 Tim. 4:8); not I, but the most holy Paul tells the same thing. Although justice makes a leader terrible, piety makes him lovable. But the government of the republic, the security of safety, and the good of concord are more likely to be expected when the best leader chooses to be loved, not to be feared. The leader is a lovely wall of the country. But he who at all times appears to be feared with continued vigor, makes all his subjects infidels; he easily fears betrayal, he suffers it more easily: he lives as a stranger among his own people; in the end he fears as much as he is feared; and he is by no means free from this scourge of unhappiness, unless, being all meek and courteous, he has learned to himself, when he judges another, to say: Do not be just too much.

THE SEVENTH RULE- Remember that you are a Christian.

19. Remember that you are a Christian, the more easily you can keep the commandments of Christ. For Christ, teaching meekness, also moderated the justice of the law; distinguishing the law and the Gospel by this distinction. And since it was not lawful to kill in the law, it will not be lawful to be angry in the Gospel. For in the law adultery was forbidden; in the Gospel, even seeing a woman to lust is judged to be a part of the committed adultery. In law, a

certificate of divorce was sufficient to separate the spouses; in the Gospel, without the crime of fornication, no cause for the division of a marriage is permitted. The law forbade swearing falsely; He ordered the Gospel not to swear at all. The law, establishing the method of revenge, said to the ancients: An eye for an eye, a tooth for a tooth (Lev. 22:20); But Christ did not want the disciples of the Gospel to wait for vengeance, but when he had been struck once, he warned him to turn the other cheek. A thousand miles he enjoined the wretched to walk two miles, forbidding retaliation in every way. The law allowed hatred to be repaid to enemies, but permitted love to friends; But the sacred precept of the Gospel: Love your enemies, he says; do good to those who hate you; and pray for those who persecute and slander you (Matt. 5:44). And when the Gospel had shown that he excelled in these greater virtues, he recalled the Christian from vainglory, and challenged him to the mercy of which only God is witness. Also, giving the rule of prayer at the same time as the words to the believers, he bound those who pray with this condition, that whoever asks to be relieved of his own debts, must confess that he is giving to another's: he will receive nothing from the Lord, if he is willing to pay nothing to his fellow-servant. Because the simplicity of the fasting Christian appeases the just judge; and to gather wealth there, where the heart is commanded to have it, that is, in heaven, where it hastens to dwell, not on earth, from which it migrates every day: it will remain entirely in darkness, unless the intention of its mind, like the eye of the body, shines simply to enlighten the members of good works. Now, indeed, he is admonished not to serve two masters, not to think of tomorrow, not to judge, lest he be judged; He is guilty of seeing the mote in his brother's eye, but not seeing the beam in his own. and he is commanded not to give the holy thing to dogs, not to dare to cast pearls before swine; asking that he may receive, seeking that he may find, knocking that it may be opened to him: it is shown by many ways and reasons how much the Christian ought to take care of a laudable purpose, that he may not be seen to err in it, worthy of such a term.

20. Therefore, as the intention recurs through the details which we inserted above from the Gospel, when the power of a leader compels you to draw your sword from its scabbard, remember that you are a Christian, who is not allowed to be angry with his brother without cause; and think longer, lest the vengeance which you see to be inflicted should pass the just measure. For if it is wrong for

a Christian to be angry, it is much more to kill. So therefore punish the guilty, leader Christiane, that by smiting mercifully, you desire to destroy not the man, but the vice; and to preserve the public discipline, lest it should perish, when the accused is guilty, to preserve the haste. Remember your faith everywhere, as in avoiding evildoers, so in correcting crimes. Indeed, the greatest power usually relaxes itself for the punishment of sin, whenever false happiness itself becomes greater unhappiness; so that because no one dares to stop him who commits crimes, either he wills what is lawful, or everything he wills is thought to be lawful. Therefore, with such temptations throbbing the mind, although the dignity of honor is available, and a numerous family of clients; although it may be that the sinner is praised in the desires of his soul, and he who behaves unjustly is blessed, climbing over the mirror of self-control, remember that you are a Christian. See that seeing to lust is a part of Christian adultery. Let the blessed Apostle tell you: God will judge fornicators and adulterers (Heb. 13:4). Let Job say, tested and not tested: For great anger and a fire burning on every side (Job. 31:12) to covet another's wife. Let the most holy Paul say again: Do you not know that your bodies are members of Christ? Taking away the members of Christ, shall I make the members of a harlot (1 Cor. 6:15)? For, warned by these words, you will be able to return easily from the precipice of pleasure. Now, whenever you swear by Almighty God, compelled to do so perhaps by the great necessity of the republic, you will at least remember to beware of perjury, if at all you could escape the oath. Remember therefore, remember that you are a Christian: carrying on the soldiery of a leader laudably, so that by frequent favors you may make many friends for yourself, whom it is commanded to love your enemies. Be more kind than severe: for this is the only perfect praise of the best leader, forget always to insult, so that truly through this energy of the seventh virtue, while you always say to yourself: Remember that you are a Christian, you deserve to live happily in this world and in the future, where it will be given the perpetual rule of the Christian leaders.

The Scriptorium Project is the work of a small group of lay people of various apostolic churches who are interested in the preservation, transmission, and translation of the works of the early and medieval church. Our efforts are to make the works of the church fathers accessible to anyone who might have an interest in Christian antiquities and the theological, philosophical, and moral writings that have become the bedrock of Western Civilization.

To-date, our releases have pulled from the Greek, Syriac, Georgian, Latin, Celtic, Ethiopian, and Coptic traditions of Christianity, and have been pulled from sundry local traditions and languages.

www.ingramcontent.com/pod-product-compliance
Lightning Source LLC
LaVergne TN
LVHW061600070526
838199LV00077B/7118